HONEYTRAPS
& SEXPIONAGE

RICHARD MARTINEZ

HONEYTRAPS AND SEXPIONAGE

Summersdale Publishers Ltd
46 West Street
Chichester
West Sussex
PO19 1RP
UK

www.summersdale.com

Printed and bound in Great Britain

ISBN: 978-1-84024-756-5

Substantial discounts on bulk quantities of Summersdale books are available to corporations, professional associations and other organisations. For details telephone Summersdale Publishers on (+44-1243-771107), fax (+44-1243-786300) or email (nicky@summersdale.com).

HONEYTRAPS & SEXPIONAGE

CONFESSIONS OF A PRIVATE INVESTIGATOR

RICHARD MARTINEZ

summersdale

ABOUT THE AUTHOR

Brought up in a single parent family, Richard Martinez joined the Air Training Corps at 13. By 20 he had achieved the Gold Duke of Edinburgh Award, an advanced gliding certificate, an RAF flying scholarship, a powered private pilot's licence and had been awarded Runner-up Best Air Cadet in the UK.

He had also played for the London Olympians American football team as a wide receiver. At the age of 21 he was commissioned as an officer in the RAF reserves, until the age of 29 when he concentrated on running his own private investigations business, Expedite Private Detective Agency, which he does to the present day, often speaking on local/national radio about his various truth-finding services. Based just outside London, he recently wrote and recorded a honeytrap song now available on iTunes.

CONTENTS

INTRODUCTION

He notices her as soon as she walks in. He looks up as she sweeps past him, and at the sight of her he catches his breath slightly. The first thing he notices is how tiny she appears; her figure in the tight little black dress is so slender, skinny even. And yet her breasts have just enough swell to grab his attention and as she passes his eyes linger on her small yet inviting hips.

Balancing on the edge of her stool at the bar, she sips delicately from her glass of sparkling water enjoying the feeling of self-assurance that fills her; an inner confidence that took years to achieve. She basks in the knowledge that she has the power to attract almost anyone around her. And yet she only has eyes for one man.

Turning from the bar, she catches him staring. He smiles and she quickly looks away. He isn't handsome or particularly rugged. He doesn't even have a good physique, but she just knows she has to find out whether he wants her before the night is over. Feigning an interest in the trivial attempts at conversation coming from the barman, she keeps her peripheral vision locked on the man filling the armchair in the corner of the room. She crosses and uncrosses her legs whenever she feels his attention wandering elsewhere and by doing this secures his concentration for well over half an hour. His eyes stay fixed on her.

As time creeps on she begins to feel a little impatient. When is he going to make a move? Or will he simply be satisfied with staring at her legs all evening? Perhaps a little more encouragement is needed? A nudge in the right direction... Reaching for her drink, she fakes a small gasp from her full, glossed lips as she sweeps her open handbag from the bar and watches its contents fall to the floor. Bending over to retrieve her belongings, her honey-blonde head almost collides with his as he dashes over to the rescue. She thanks him politely.

An hour later there is hardly any distance between the newly acquainted couple. He has bought her several drinks and as his eyes focus on her chest she undoes another button of her dress to reveal a little more cleavage. His eyes fixate on the delicate dance of her fingers on the fabric and widen as she exposes the top of her bra and just enough flesh to tease him.

And then it's over. She tells him she must leave. She has an early appointment in the morning and can't risk oversleeping. She extricates herself from his arms, one of which is placed across her lower back, almost touching her bottom, the other resting on her right hip. He has spent the past fifteen minutes delicately stroking her there.

Suddenly there is tension in the air, a few moments when neither of them knows how to deal with her departure. Then comes the moment she's been waiting for. He asks for her number, tells her he thinks she is beautiful and that he wants her. Boldness overtakes him enough to tell her he wants to sleep with her. Well, it makes it simpler that way. There is no doubt in her mind that he will contact her the following day and equally, there will be no doubt left in his wife's mind when the evening's events are replayed before her eyes.

She works for me, the slender-framed woman in the little black dress. My name is Richard Martinez and I am a private detective.

It was fiction author Paul Auster who wrote, 'The detective is the one who unlocks, who listens... in effect, the writer and the detective are interchangeable.'

In the chapters that follow I am going to give you an insight into the secret world of private investigations. I enjoy the secrecy of my work. Unravelling the twisted skeins of tangled relationships is part of my business and gives me a unique vantage point into the intricacies of people's lives.

There is something cathartic about watching and becoming part of other people's pain, as often happens in carrying out my tasks as an investigator; I have seen many hearts break before my very eyes. As a consequence I feel I have come to know myself more in the past ten years, since I began practising as a detective, than ever before.

I will be opening the door to a private world, giving an insight into some of the dirtiest secrets to be found in boardrooms and bedrooms across the country. To quote Sherlock Holmes, 'The world is full of obvious things which no one, by chance, ever observes.' What has amazed and sometimes shocked me over the past ten years is the depths some people will sink to and the enormity of impacts that the actions of a few have on many.

As you read this book you will become aware of the many diverse, startling and, reluctantly I have to admit, ingenious tactics utilised by some people to get what they want. Hopefully the result is an entertaining and thought-provoking read on a little-known subject.

I have changed names, dates and descriptions of some places to protect my clients' right to anonymity and privacy, but the main events are true, incredible as many of them seem. I won't be spinning you any yarns. What is written on these pages is true to the very last letter.

I have a natural inbred yearning to unearth the truth, and the truth is often stranger than anything imagined by an inventive crime novelist. Although the public's appetite for intrigue is satiated by lurid and exaggerated tales of the exploits of private eyes, the fictional tales contain unbelievable untruths. The PI is constantly misrepresented in fiction and on the big screen. My aim is to reveal the facts behind my work.

It's a common myth that we PIs spend most of our days swilling bourbon and dabbling in messy divorce cases. Many of my cases involve love, intrigue and tangled webs, but I also get involved in a wide variety of other cases. And while it remains a certain requirement of my job to stay in the shadows, I am keen to open the door a little on my private world. What you'll glimpse behind is raw but honest.

I have spent the past ten years witnessing the essence of human drama unfold before my eyes. It has been an honour to work so closely with so many clients. Through my work as a PI I have been able to reach out and, I believe, help a number of people, some of whom were trapped in desperately unhappy and sometimes dangerous situations through no fault of their own. My knowledge and expertise has unearthed information that has had far-reaching effects on the lives of others.

As my experience has grown I've become increasingly intelligent in an emotional sense and, perhaps for the first time in my life, I am truly able to understand the pain of other people. I feel it with them. More often than not the pain has been caused by either a cheat or a control freak.

Do I feel guilty about revealing the truth and becoming a catalyst for what are sometimes monumental changes in the lives of others? Not at all, not for a second. While I believe that my insight into the private lives of others has allowed my empathy to develop and grow to a greater depth than ever before, I still believe that you reap what you sow. Your mission, should you choose to accept it, is to join me in gaining an insight into the world of liars and cheats.

This book is not a collection of tales to warm the heart; it's not chocolate for the soul. Don't continue to read if you're a little prudish; it's not a book about sex but some of the tales involve lurid and extreme detail. Put the book down if you're easily disturbed; this is not a book about blood, gore and violence but, sadly, some of my clients have endured far too many years locked in a cycle of misery and fear.

I was attracted to the world of investigating through my need for excitement and variety. I've always been a bit of an adrenaline junkie and my career in the RAF as a flying officer was something that could satisfy this need, for a while at least. I knew I could handle most situations, as I look after myself. That's not to say that women can't or don't make equally as effective PIs, it's just that some of the situations I have come across over the past ten years have required a fair amount of physical strength. If I had to choose a partner to accompany me on a 'job' I would probably choose a woman since they have an innate ability to sense what's going on around them. Their intuition can be invaluable in my line of work and, as I mention in the chapter on infidelity, their gut feeling is almost always accurate. They also have the ability to 'talk down' a situation; most men don't. Moving through each chapter, you will discover some of the covert methods used in unearthing 'dirty little secrets'.

As for job satisfaction, what exactly are the rewards of being a private sleuth? Well, I believe there are many. For starters, it can be financially rewarding. I always had a burning ambition to build my own business and be my own boss, as my father has done all his life. It's certainly not a career to bring huge wealth, though I can't grumble. It has definitely brought me what is more valuable in my eyes: a great number of friends and many exciting escapades. It's a job that takes me all over the country and sometimes out of it too. I've also had the honour of playing a small part in 'rescuing' some young men from potentially lethal situations and some women from a circle of abuse and violence. Such is the reward of the PI.

And while many a young schoolboy dreams of becoming a detective (although I realise these days footballer and rock star remain top of the tree), it has to be said that the profession of PI in general has always been held in disrepute. I feel this is grossly unfair; every profession hosts a small number of black sheep. It's a pity that we're all tarred with the same brush. The majority of us are highly dedicated professionals, many with police or military backgrounds, working alongside rather than against the law. Many established detective agencies such as my own make a point of giving first refusal of vacancies to retired police officers.

I can put my hand on my heart and say truthfully that I have never done anything I am ashamed of over the past ten years; there is nothing I would be afraid to disclose, save the personal details of my clients and their private affairs.

Today my agency is thriving and business has never been better. I believe that's partly because the service I offer my clients is valued and appreciated. My office may not be as prominent as some of the PI firms located in affluent areas such as Mayfair, but the lower rent where I am based just outside London means I can afford to keep my fees competitive. And although I don't have as many staff to answer my phones as the central London firms, at least my phones are ringing.

When I first started out I had little idea of what my future career would hold; I suppose I had a stereotypical image of the traditional US private dick. The term 'private investigator' conjures, to the uninitiated, an image of romanticism mixed with dangerous excitement. It appears to be the sort of role played by mysterious strangers clad in long raincoats, moving stealthily along dimly lit corners of rain-drenched backstreets.

So what is the reality? How exactly does a PI spend his days (and nights)? Am I a civilian spy, stirred by a sense of curiosity and justice? Do I spend my time mixing with beautiful women and unscrupulous businessmen in an effort to foil and outwit their schemes to gain financial or political power?

The truth is that my work is, at times, monotonous (endless surveillance), sometimes dangerous, often highly emotionally charged and, as I hope to demonstrate, it offers me a unique insight into the human psyche. I do gain immense satisfaction from the knowledge that my work brings justice and peace of mind to many of my clients.

In the words of Albert Einstein, 'The most beautiful thing we can experience is the mysterious', and I do love my 'mysterious' job. How else would I get to meet lunatics and conmen, narcissists, bigamists, adulterers, sociopaths, petty thieves, outright criminals and pathological liars in an average day at the office?

1

LET ME GIVE YOU MY CARD…

Do you recall the petite lady in the little black dress back on page 1? Her name is Kim and, as I said, she works for me. Kim lives a double life in some respects. Standing at the school gates in the morning she waves her two young children off to school before dashing off to her part-time job or the gym. The rest of the day is spent catching up on housework and shopping until it's time for school pick-up.

Once or twice a week she arranges for her mum to babysit and prepares herself for an evening out, all expenses paid. Taking great care to get ready, she slips into a hot bath with some sweet-smelling oil, and gets dressed into something a little bit slinky, not too tarty.

She relishes the thought of locating and working on her target for the evening and enjoys even more the knowledge that she'll earn herself a tidy sum for her free night out, usually in the region of £150. Kim is not a man-hater; on the contrary, she enjoys the company of men, but like many people she can't bear cheats. This has more than a little something to do with the fact that she lived alongside a cheat for the last three years of her marriage and now struggles to bring her child up alone as a result of finding out the truth. She is an ex-client of mine who came to me in a terrible state a few years ago, heavily pregnant and more than a little suspicious of her 'always at the office' husband. We arranged for Lily, an attractive, slim, blonde lady, to stand alone at the bar of his local and within the first hour he was taking down her telephone number and asking if she'd like to spend the following evening with him.

At the time, Kim was devastated to say the least; apart from his frequent absences from home they had a happy marriage, or so she thought. Remarkably, they remained friends after the divorce and, according to Kim, he says he was very much in love with her, happy in his marriage and looking forward to becoming a father, but when temptation came his way he just couldn't help himself. I guess, for Kim, being a honeytrapper gives her a sense of regaining the power that was taken from her during that time in her life. And it gives her the cash she needs to give her children a good lifestyle.

I regularly send girls out on honeytrapping missions; my busiest times being holiday seasons – midsummer in particular. I have a feeling this is to do with the flimsy summer dresses girls wear at this time of year and the bare, tanned skin on display. Women want to feel they can trust their man around temptation. The Christmas period means lots more alcohol and, again, doubts about a partner's fidelity in tempting situations start to arise.

And it's not just suspicious wives who set a honeytrap goddess on to an unsuspecting man either. According to the Director General of MI5, Jonathan Evans, there is a growing threat of state-sponsored espionage from China, whose government is eager to obtain intelligence against vital parts of Britain's economy, including the computer systems of big banks and financial service companies.

Towards the end of 2008, during a trip to China with Gordon Brown, a senior Downing Street adviser and top aide to the Prime

Minister had his BlackBerry phone stolen after being picked up by a Chinese woman. It happened on the second day of the trip when Downing Street staff went to a hotel disco to relax and enjoy themselves for the evening. A lively party was in full swing, with several hundred people present. Lots of people crowded together on the dance floor and the senior aide was approached by an attractive woman. They spent a couple of hours together, dancing and chatting, before she joined him in his hotel room. They spent the night together. In the morning, once she'd left him alone, he realised his BlackBerry was missing and had the embarrassing task of reporting the incident to the Prime Minister's Special Branch protection team.

He was formally reprimanded; it was strongly suspected he had fallen prey to a honeytrap operation by Chinese intelligence agents. Although all Downing Street BlackBerrys are password protected, most are not encrypted and therefore the secrets they contain, whether stored data or sent and received emails, are easily obtained by a good hacker. Experts feared that even if the BlackBerry didn't contain top secret information, it might enable a hostile intelligence service to hack into the Downing Street server.

I'm sure the aide is exceptionally relieved his name never made the papers. It's embarrassing enough to find that the girl you've spent the night with only had eyes for your mobile, without having potentially revealed state secrets.

Of course, I'll be naming no names but I've had a fair bit of business come my way from wives and husbands of our friends in Westminster. Long hours and endless opportunities are to blame – spending more time at the office than at home leads to bonking in the boardroom. It's the same in any profession where home life often takes a back seat: doctors, police officers, judges... One of my most recent cases involved a judge. We'll call him Paul to protect the innocent. He presides at a Crown Court in one of the Home Counties.

It's one of those unusual days in summer, sweltering hot but not stiflingly humid. A day when the last thing you want to be doing is pushing a pen around a desk. I work until lunchtime, then head over to Richmond Park to meet an old school friend, Liz.

We meet at the café next to the cycle-hire shop at Roehampton Gate. I haven't had time for breakfast, and they serve the most delicious tuna melt panini in London. Liz is waiting for me at a table inside and has ordered a latte with vanilla flavouring. She can read me like a book; she knows I'll turn up precisely on time (my RAF training again) and vanilla latte is my favourite, even on a day with temperature in the mid-nineties. It's going to be a very pleasant afternoon – I'm going to reward myself with the rest of the day off. I've made up my mind.

Within seconds of taking my seat, Liz launches into a mega-soap tale of the dramas afflicting all of our old school friends and I chuckle to myself; everything was a drama for her during our schooldays in Streatham. Some people never change – it's very refreshing. What you see is what you get with Liz, something I don't find in abundance in my job. I've learnt to assume nothing and question everything. But with old friends I know I can relax.

Just as I'm polishing off the last mouthful of delicious lemon meringue pie and cream, Liz winks at me suggestively.

'I will if you will.'

'We can't do that on a full stomach, can we?'

'Of course, it's just what we need after all that pie and I can catch you up on the rest of the news on the way round – we'll hire them for three hours, it'll be fab.'

I have to admit I could do with the exercise since I haven't so much as looked at a gym for over a week now. I've spent most of that time either stuck behind the wheel of my car on surveillance tasks or behind my desk completing reports or conducting research. Research is an important element of my work and one of my first tasks when taking on a new case. An intelligence file is every investigator's vital first tool. Basic background information can usually be gleaned from the client who, if they're a spouse, will be able to provide most personal details. I enjoy assembling a profile, building a mental image of the target, their motivations, movements, their history. It's then a case of adding each new piece of the jigsaw until the full picture emerges and the case is solved. The only drawback with research is the hours I spend sitting on my backside.

I put on a cycle helmet and Liz tries her best to get her leg over one of the only bicycles left in the hire shed; the beautiful weather seems to have given half of London the idea to cruise around the park on a bike. But since she's no more than five foot one, including her trainers and cycle helmet, Liz is having a few problems.

'My bloody seat is too high!'

I give the Indian chap who works in the cycle shed an apologetic nod.

'You can take the girl out of Streatham, but...'

Finally hauling herself on, Liz ignores my muffled guffaws and we set off in the direction of the Royal Ballet School at White Lodge.

'Do you remember Hazel Mundle? She used to be in our class.'

'Vaguely, yes. I think I used to pull her pigtails.'

'You pulled everyone's pigtails! Anyway, you'll never guess who I saw her with the other day...'

My phone rings. Liz stops abruptly and falls off her seat, cursing loudly. As I answer she gives me an accusatory stare; she knows I won't ignore the call and as I don my hands free and prepare to continue the ride while chatting to 'Sandra', the lady on the other end of the line, I'm aware of Liz's eyes boring into the back of my head.

It's my intention to take Sandra's number and call her later this evening, but it's clear she's not a lady who wants to wait so I decide I may as well let her pour out her heart as I continue to cycle and

I'll make it up to Liz later with a huge frothy cappuccino. She's like me – easily pleased. I can tell from the urgency in Sandra's voice that she's reached a point where she needs to do something about her situation and do something *now*. I have visions of her pacing for hours building herself up to making this call because I have barely announced my name when she launches into her story. It seems she has spent the last five years of her life more or less in constant misery. All she ever wanted was to be a homemaker and when she met Paul she fell for him immediately. He was everything she wanted in a man: ambitious, hardworking and a wonderful provider. She spent her days keeping a beautiful home and lovingly preparing his evening meal. After five years of marriage she began to suspect he spent some of his time with other women, although he would try to convince her that men in his position, as a judge, have no choice but to work long hours and she had better get used to it. Desperate to avoid the humiliation of a failed marriage, she stuck with him and made every effort to keep Paul satisfied, thinking this was the way to win back his attention and 'out' the other women.

With her constant attentions and efforts to seduce him unsuccessful, the adoration she felt for him dwindled and she became more and more unhappy. Her efforts to prove his infidelity were never successful; his prominence led him to be very careful and he was a slick operator. But by instinct, she could always tell when he was seeing someone and when it came to an end. On ending an affair he would begin to show more interest in her and would become less critical. In the earlier years of their marriage she was so relieved to have 'won' him back she made the most of the attention, optimistic that if she worked hard he wouldn't stray again. Nowadays his fickle nature sickened her. All she now wanted was a way out of a bad situation and some leverage to obtain a very healthy divorce settlement.

It seems Paul is of the opinion that women who stay at home shouldn't have any stake in the property or finances of a marriage since they've never 'worked' for it, so she knows he will fight to keep every penny he's built up over his career. Sandra figured that after five years of being cheated on she had more than 'earned' her right to a sizeable chunk of their property. What she now needed was evidence of his infidelity. Since she was convinced he had just finished with a rather plain, skinny PA who recently joined his team, it wasn't particularly good timing for her to approach me, but his nonchalant manner when she questioned him about her suspicions was the straw that broke the camel's back. It quickly becomes apparent she can't bear the thought of delaying just one more day, let alone long enough for him to take a new mistress.

'I need to do something now while I've still got the strength – I feel like I'm sinking, Mr Martinez.'

We discuss the options and decide the best way to obtain proof that Paul is not a faithful husband is to force his hand a little. When I say 'force' I don't by any shadow of a doubt mean coerce him into behaviour he would otherwise avoid; I simply mean hand him an opportunity and let him decide what to do about it. The only difference between a simple evening out and a honeytrap is that I will be there filming the events as they unfold. The fact that I'm there secretly filming events will not alter Paul's behaviour, nor anyone else's. A faithful husband will not chat up and take the phone number of a beautiful woman in a bar, full stop, whether I'm sitting in the corner or not.

Sandra agrees with the honeytrap, but has no idea where her husband will be from one day to the next, so is unable to give me a location to send my employee to. Paul gave up telling Sandra his movements years ago, and only calls her during the day if he wants his dry-cleaning collected or another errand run.

'That's no problem, Mrs Bridgeford.'

'Oh please call me Sandra, it seems crazy to remain formal since I've just told you a secret I've kept to myself for the past five years.'

A tight laugh escapes from her throat and she sounds very girlie for a moment. 'I haven't even told my mother.'

'Believe me, Sandra, I've heard pretty much everything. Don't worry about shocking me.'

'Yes, I can believe that, but it is all so embarrassing. If you'd told me I'd be arranging something like this ten years ago I'd have thought you were out of your mind.'

'I know. My dad always said we should live our lives backwards. That way we'd understand everything a lot better, you know, not make so many mistakes. But you mustn't feel embarrassed or bad about all this, Sandra. All you're doing is taking a little control back. Everyone has a right to control over their own life, don't they? You have a right to make your own decisions and so does Paul. If he makes the wrong decision and I capture the evidence, there's no one to blame but him, agreed?'

I agree to call in on Sandra on my way home and as I take down her address I'm amazed to find it's located about three minutes' drive away from Robin Hood Gate, on the south side of Richmond Park. I need to take basic details from her such as the make, model and registration of her husband's car, and so on, as it helps if I get as much personal information as possible at the outset. As our conversation ends I realise Liz and I have covered lots of ground; I spot the beautiful ballet school, originally a hunting lodge for King George I, just ahead. To our left is the lake, nestling at the bottom of the hill.

Liz stares at me in anticipation, anxious for me to fill in the blanks for her. She's heard one half of the conversation, cycling so close to me during my phone conversation I could almost swear we were riding a tandem. But she already suspects I won't fill her in on all the lurid details; she knows me better than that. Client confidentiality is paramount in my book – my clients come from all walks of life and I have enough stories of the rich, powerful and celebrity to fill the front pages of *News of the World* for a good few weeks, but I'm paid to get the job done efficiently and discreetly and that's what I do, even when I am with my oldest friends.

'If I tell you I'll have to kill you.'

Liz laughs and accepts the brush-off with good humour. I've had girlfriends who find it difficult to tolerate the fact that I keep my work private – they expect me to tell them everything, but I don't work that way. A pilot who sings risks his wings and all that. I was schooled in the art of self-discipline in the RAF and it soon becomes second nature.

Bang goes my afternoon off. It can be tricky to take a holiday in my profession. You can plan all the leave you like, but when a call comes in it's difficult to ignore – it's not like running a building or decorating business where you can book clients in advance. When someone calls me they've usually reached the end of their tether. And yes, I know I'm my own boss, but something in me finds it difficult to turn away someone needing help.

Arriving at the house, I take a clipboard and pen from my car: standard props for one of my well-used ruses of a workman providing an estimate of some sort. It's a smokescreen that should cover Sandra, should any nosy neighbours have a word with Paul over the garden fence, although the nearest house is actually more than twenty feet away. A high wall surrounds the house, giving the impression of a fortress. Well, 'house' is actually a misnomer – anyone I know would call it a mansion. The black wrought-iron gates probably cost more than most of the houses in town where I live. I push the buzzer at the side of one of the gates and they swing inwards, operated by remote control. I enter the porch and swing the brass knocker shaped as a lion's head against the dark, oak door. Now this is the kind of door I need at my house – it's definitely high enough to afford me entry without ducking. I can tell by the echoing bang there is a whole lot of space in the hallway beyond. Moments later the door is opened by Sophia.

Sandra is one of those people who defy one of the unwritten laws of nature: people should be blessed with money or good looks, not both. She would be considered a remarkable-looking woman in any circumstance. I think she must be pushing six feet tall – she stands almost on a level with me, even in her bare feet. But in spite of her height she is soft-looking, almost delicate, with her light-brown hair falling loosely, framing her face with the tousled curls associated with childhood. I guess she is in her thirties at most, although she has the sort of classic beauty that defies age – she could be fifty. Whatever her age she is startlingly beautiful. Her eyes are pale blue and quite piercing, giving her an intense look and with her chiselled and prominent cheekbones she emits an elegant, assured kind of beauty.

'Good afternoon, Sandra.' I shake her proffered hand firmly. Sandra smiles, displaying two cute dimples at the corners of her mouth as she does so, making her beauty all the more impressive. She is dressed casually, in light-grey slacks and a pale-pink pullover, but there is nothing casual in her demeanour. Her face is taut and as she welcomes me in I feel tension in the air.

I follow Sandra into the hall and our journey through the house into the sitting room is an education in understated elegance. Paintings adorn the walls, spaced at tasteful intervals, and although I don't know enough about art to comment intelligently I get the feeling that anyone who does would get very excited about these pieces. Our sitting-room destination is a large, high-ceilinged room with tall windows along one wall and dual-aspect patio doors overlooking a huge and beautifully maintained garden. Sandra gestures for me to sit in one of the armchairs positioned at the side of a large, deep sofa and I can almost visualise the rope barrier as I sit down, feeling slightly guilty for ruffling the perfect cushions. Sandra told me during our telephone conversation there are no children from the marriage and I get the feeling it's a saving grace: children wouldn't thrive in a house like this. I feel like I'm visiting a National Trust property.

Having been so chatty on the phone it surprises me to find Sandra reluctant to talk now we're face to face. I'm relieved for her that she's already told me her main worries – now all we need to do is get down to business.

She studies me with an intense scrutiny not usually borne well in adults and I feel tempted to shuffle around a little.

'You can trust me, Sandra, I promise you that.'

Her stare softens and she visibly relaxes. I get the feeling she's checked me out and she's reasonably happy she's in safe hands. When it comes to initial encounters, most people base their decision on whether they can trust someone on the briefest of interactions; basically, first impressions count. I have found it possible to give an impression of power and capability before ever uttering a word. Initial information is weighted far more heavily than anything that comes later. If you engage in the first few minutes as a warm, honest, positive person that is the lasting impression you will leave them with.

'I've been thinking, Sandra, it's a shame you have no idea where your husband goes after work – it means I can only arrange a honeytrap by following him myself until he goes to an appropriate place.'

'Couldn't we track his movements?'

'I could provide you with a tracker if you'd like, but you would have to plant it – are you happy to do that?'

'I wouldn't know how to.'

'I can show you how, but I can't fit one to someone's property without their permission. It would be an infringement of their rights – I work strictly within the law.'

'That's all right then!' Sandra looks delighted 'Paul is using my car this week – his Jaguar is in the garage.'

Sandra happens to know that Paul has a dentist appointment at 4 p.m. this afternoon, since he asked her to book it for him. I take the details and decide to fit the device as soon as I leave her

– I should make it to the address just in time to place the tracker under the vehicle while Paul has some root canal treatment, and he'll be none the wiser. A tracker will allow us to quickly build up a picture of Paul's 'true' life and send in a honeytrapper at the earliest opportunity. Using a tracker saves me many surveillance hours and ultimately is gentler on the client's pocket.

Most spouses generally have an idea of their other half's favourite haunts and couples are usually aware of their respective girls' or boys' nights out well in advance, so landing a honeytrapper into the picture, in the right place at the right time, is simple. In Sandra's case, her relationship with her husband has grown evermore distant with them living almost parallel lives. Without the use of a tracker I'd have to follow him, possibly for days, until I could set a honeytrapper in place.

I often advise the use of a GPS tracker system to anyone who phones the office for advice but can't afford to employ my services. I can provide the equipment for them to purchase and they can follow the daily movements of their husband or wife from dawn until dusk. It's a method of integrity testing and can often expose a liar before a week is out. Every address their spouse visits, every jewellery shop or motel, can be monitored from the comfort of their own home.

Sandra sounded so desperate I think the quicker we get down to business the better. Normally, I would provide the tracker to the spouse and allow them to do what they will with it, but since Paul is using Sandra's car for the week from tomorrow (he has booked his Jaguar XF in at a specialist garage), I have the authority to plant one myself. It's Sandra's car – if she wants a tracker fitted she can jolly well have one as far as I'm concerned.

As I rise to leave, Sandra's eyes fill with tears. 'How long before it's all over, Richard?'

She blushes instantly, unaccustomed to revealing her vulnerability to a stranger. All the muscles tighten in her jaw in her efforts to regain control, and she does so brilliantly in my opinion. I assure her I'll work on wrapping things up quickly. I find many clients are in a desperate rush to get things sorted as soon as possible. They're usually going through a rough time and want to move through it fast but magic bullets don't exist in the real world. Everyone loves a shortcut, but shortcuts often lead in the wrong direction.

I arrive at Robin Park Lane a few minutes after 4 p.m. and cruise along until I spot Sandra's Range Rover, sandwiched between a red Montego and a metallic-blue Vauxhall Astra. Paul may be a bad husband, but he is damn talented at manoeuvring – the Range Rover appears to have been airlifted into the space, it's almost touching the Astra, but it gives me a bit more cover from passing vehicles so I'm not complaining. I don my blue overcoat before I make my way over, looking every bit the old-fashioned mechanic out on an emergency breakdown mission – another of my master disguises. I lie on the pavement, my head under the body of the vehicle, and fit the tracker within seconds. Fortunately I'm away before I have to answer any awkward questions from passersby.

I retire to a nearby fast-food restaurant, where I enjoy a jumbo cup of coffee and wait for the tracking receiver to tell me my target is on the move. It takes a while, and I begin to wonder if Paul is getting a totally new set of teeth fitted, but after just over an hour the tracker detects movement. I track the car for twenty minutes or so, watching the red dot occasionally pause, presumably at traffic lights or junctions, before zipping along the city streets. Suddenly, the dot comes to an abrupt stop on Cleveland Street – a part of town filled with upmarket bars and restaurants. Then it vanishes. I'm guessing Paul has pulled into an underground car park, which means I can't get a GPS signal.

Within five minutes I've found the only underground car park in the vicinity and am hoping it's the same one as Paul chose. I quickly locate his car and then coast my motorbike into a space nearby. Soon I'm on the street, casually eyeing the clientele in the various hostelries and restaurants enjoying their after-work Martinis. Luckily it's not long before I spot a man I believe to be Paul, sitting in a cocktail bar wearing a rather severe, long black coat. He's perched cross-legged on a bar stool, and sips an amber-coloured spirit from a heavy tumbler.

A quick check of the photo in my pocket confirms my suspicions: it's Paul, all right. He isn't with anybody, so I text Kim – who has already confirmed her availability as a honeytrapper tonight – and ask her to get her firmly toned backside to the bar as quickly as possible. Then I walk casually inside, take a seat in the corner, order an alcohol-free cocktail and wait for the impending fireworks.

Not too long afterwards I receive a text from Kim. She is nearby. I reply to her text describing what Paul is wearing and where he is sitting. When Kim clicks into the bar in her silver-tipped stilettos and tight pencil skirt, every man turns to look. I smile to myself: she looks perfect. Every inch the sophisticated, well-dressed legal secretary; her outfit brief for the evening. She casts her eye around the bar, as if she's looking for a friend, but apparently having no joy she seats herself next to Paul and orders a Sunset Island. Good girl, she's sticking to my honeytrap rules – strictly no alcohol on duty. Only someone who knew what she was up to would have noticed her gaze lingering for just a second longer on Paul than any of the other bar clientele before she sat down. I watch her in one of the mirrors on the wall. She glances around the bar again and includes me in her sweep. I tug at one of my ears. This is a recognised signal between us to indicate she has sat near the right man.

It's an intimate venue, and from my vantage point I can hear and see everything. And of course, film everything too with a zoom-lens DVD recorder hidden inside my rucksack. Kim begins to hunt in her handbag, and knocks a packet of tissues to the floor – apparently without noticing.

'Here, allow me.'

Paul, ever the gentleman, leans down by Kim's long tanned legs and passes her back the packet.

'Oh! Thank you.' Kim gives him a lovely smile. 'I'm a bit flustered! I'm supposed to meet a friend here, but I am late. I am worried she may have left already but I left my mobile at home in my hurry to leave my flat so I don't know if she has tried to contact me.' She looks coy, waiting for him to say something. But he simply gives her a polite nod and resumes his previous position: legs crossed, looking out of the window – heavy tumbler balanced on his pin-striped knee.

The bar is starting to fill up now, and the crowd is clearly a fashionable bunch – or want to be. There are plenty of elaborate haircuts, garish shirts and brightly coloured accessories, and Paul looks very out-of-place in his dark coat, with his clipped, grey hair and sensible suit. He observes the crowd like a man wistfully watching a play and wishing he were one of the characters. I get the feeling he wants to join the revelry but he's just far too sensible. Or perhaps I'm looking at someone having a mid-life crisis.

I employ a number of very attractive and alluring women as honeytraps for male targets. We find that only a handful of men actually resist their many charms, while 90 per cent fall straight into the trap. I provide the member of my team with a photo so that they can identify the right person, but I don't bother with any of the other details. Men fall for looks rather than deep, meaningful conversation and they're usually snared within the hour.

My female honeytrappers find it quite disturbing just how easily men take the bait. They start the evening confident that the guy they are chatting with is too nice to stray and usually end the evening successful, but disappointed. Some get a real rush from doing it though – I find these are the ones who have been hurt in the same way by their previous partner(s) and so they thoroughly enjoy rooting out other love cheats and exposing them and their true colours. One girl who works for me feels that the pain of suspecting a partner is much worse than the pain when they know the truth. I can understand that way of thinking. And they often think that the slimy men who make lurid suggestions to them within minutes deserve all the trouble they get.

My top priority when sending a female honeytrap out on a job is her safety. She wears a tiny microphone taped to her body and always stays in a busy public place. The microphone has to be small because of the slinky dresses the girls wear to maximise the effect of their female curves. If the meeting between the honeytrap and the target were ever to progress physically there would be several men who would get a shock when their roving hands discovered a small electronic device tucked between the breast and Wonderbra cup of the gorgeous woman they are touching. I also make sure there is back-up nearby, within earshot, should she need any help; usually me.

When performing a sting the girl should look attractive, but not provocative. The idea is that the man initiates the conversation and makes all the moves. To begin with they have to approach the situation differently to me when I'm on a honeytrapping job. It would seem very odd if an attractive woman approached a total stranger in a bar and started feeding him compliments. The target would smell a rat immediately. Instead, she will usually drop some money or something from her bag while standing nearby, or keep looking at her watch as if she's waiting for someone to turn up. She can smile at the target and say hello, but no more than that. It remains his choice as to whether to strike up a conversation. After this she can only react to what he suggests. The honeytrapper is reactive. She won't touch, kiss or offer the target sex and she won't overdo the questioning. It's for the target to decide how far he wants to go.

The majority of men deny they're in a relationship, even deny their children, or some will say they are in the process of getting divorced. Funnily enough, they are closer than they think. The women in my team find it surprising just how convincing these men can be. I'm sure it must alter their perception when they get approached while off-duty – they feel a lot more sceptical and less willing to take things on face value. That's no bad thing, though. I think it helps them take things slowly and get to know a guy before jumping in with both feet.

In some cases the man asks for a phone number just to prove he can; men love to collect trophies. They are competitive and the competition is satisfied in some by the achievement of obtaining the phone number. The physical act of sex may not be what's important. So he may have no intention of actually contacting the girl to take things any further, but that may be small comfort to his wife who waits at home for him. It's natural for people to flirt with the opposite sex; it's for her to decide whether the level of flirting has been intolerable.

An hour passes, and Kim has done her best to lure Sandra's husband into an exchange of phone numbers, but to Paul's credit she's failed. Few men could resist a beautiful woman bestowing her most alluring 'come and get me' looks upon them without responding but he's simply not interested, and I give Kim the secret signal to say she can leave. She winks at me on the way out, and I know she's happy. She loves the few occasions when men turn her down – she says it gives her hope there are still a few good ones out there. But I'm not so sure with Paul. He was a little bit *too* cold towards Kim. Most men enjoy talking to a beautiful woman, even if they don't try and take things further. Paul's total disinterest is confusing, and I suspect there's more to him than meets the eye. Does he know he's being set up? Does he fear someone might be watching his movements? And there's something odd about his choice of bar, too. There are a few colourful characters here, to put it mildly. Considering Paul's profession, appearance and demeanour, I'd imagine he wouldn't care for the flamboyant behaviour and language of the clientele. Maybe after a day in court he needs a little colour in his life?

Almost the moment Kim leaves, Paul orders another cocktail and I guess I'm not the only one on the non-alcoholic variety. If it is alcohol, it's having the opposite effect on Paul than it does on most people. His body is becoming more tense and twitchy, and he begins to grind his teeth and breathe quickly. I nearly miss what happens next, as I study the menu and decide between two elaborately named non-alcoholic cocktails, both also elaborately priced at five pounds fifty each. Paul exits the bar in two swift strides, and within seconds is outside and moving quickly past the window.

I wait a moment, aware his sudden exit suggests he may well be onto me, then begin my pursuit. Out on the street, I see Paul disappear into the car park and within moments I'm following the Range Rover as it glides through the streets of London, heading north towards Camden. The huge corporate office blocks begin to peter out, and small shops and residential properties line the streets.

I'm beginning to suspect Paul may be headed to Hampstead Heath, which is not good news for Sandra – not good news at all. And I'm right. The Range Rover coasts down Finchley Road and towards the west side of Hampstead Heath: the notorious gay cruising area where men come for no-obligation sex with other men.

'I'm so sorry,' I tell Sandra, as tears stream down her beautiful face. I pass her a tissue.

'In a way, I knew,' Sandra says, and gives her nose a good blow. 'He's always so cold. I knew there was something more... it just wasn't other women.'

It's been a surreal morning for Sandra. She's just watched, from the comfort of her very English, very traditional family home, infrared footage of her husband giving oral sex to a man he's just met on Hampstead Heath.

Sandra was in pieces at first, but she calmed down after an hour or so and we talked over everything I'd seen and heard. She even managed to joke about her 'faithful husband' refusing Kim's many assets. 'How many clients of yours can say that?' she asked, almost with a hint of pride and I had to admit there haven't been many.

'I'll get a copy of all this sent to your solicitor,' I tell her, packing away the video footage. 'But you've all the time in the world. You don't need to action divorce proceedings until you're ready.'

'Divorce?' Sandra looks genuinely shocked. 'I'm not going to *divorce* him. What would I divorce him over? It's not as if he's seeing other women.'

'Oh... I...' I'm wrong-footed for a moment and don't know what to say.

'Things won't stay the same,' Sandra reassures me, 'but we'll stay together. I've built my life around him, Richard. And it's not as if I have any real competition.'

Each to their own, I suppose. Now Sandra knows there aren't other women involved, in some ways her dignity remains intact. She knows she's not to blame for his 'little indiscretions', and she hasn't 'failed in her wifely duties', as she puts it. Now it's clear the problem is on Paul's side, it seems she can cope with life as his wife.

Although this hasn't been a typical honeytrapping case, it always surprises me how many women stay with their partners, even after their man has been caught out by someone like Kim. You never know – in the long-term those in my profession may stabilise many relationships and prevent partners from straying. Paul was one of those rare men who wasn't bowled over by the attentions of a beautiful woman, although it had more to do with his homosexual leanings than devoted loyalty to his wife but, as use of the honeytrap increases, partners may become more cautious when flirting. After all, next time you get chatted up in a bar by a good-looking stranger will you be confident that you've

LET ME GIVE YOU MY CARD...

not fallen prey to a honeytrapper? Your partner might not be around, but they may have their private eye on you...

2

LET ME GUESS YOUR STAR SIGN...

Not one of my best chat-up lines but useful in some situations. Some may think it's a bit cheesy but on some women it works like a charm. Sometimes it works a little too well. And when an attractive woman, one that I've spent the entire evening chatting up, wants to takes things further and leans in for a kiss, my job isn't always easy. Once it gets to this point my professionalism and pride in my work require me to make my excuses and leave, and that's exactly what I do.

Fortunately, my years in the RAF instilled in me a high level of self-discipline. Few officers allow their guard to slip. I wouldn't risk my hard-fought-for reputation by indulging in a passionate clinch with my client's girlfriend/partner. As if the poor guy hasn't got enough on his plate – he has to be able to trust his private detective.

For most of my ten years in the job I have been in serious relationships. I try to bear in mind how difficult it can be for someone who is in a relationship with me when she knows that I'm heading off to chat up another woman. Usually I am able to reassure my partner that business is business, and although I spend a proportion of my working week chatting up women I'm doing it for money, not for pleasure – although more often than not I do enjoy myself.

Once I leave the house I only have eyes for one woman – my target. The price for an evening varies from around £300 to £400, and I'm regularly contacted by men who are more than willing to part with their cash to test their partner's integrity by setting up a honeytrap. They feel it's a small price to pay for peace of mind. The honeytrap has become evermore popular in recent years, partly I think because it is so easy in the Internet era for men and women to meet up for sex. A new lover is available at the click of a mouse and it makes it far more difficult for some to feel confident in a relationship.

Although I have been working as a honeytrapper for nine years, I have noticed a threefold increase in demand for this kind of work over the past year or so. It does tend to fluctuate over the year, midsummer and Christmas being my busiest times.

I find that, while women tend to book honeytraps before making a big commitment such as getting married, buying a house or having a baby, men usually make contact following whispered rumours concerning their partner through friends or family.

Once the client has made contact I try to get as much information about my female target as possible before setting off on the job. This is vital because women don't generally respond on the basis of looks alone: they are turned on much more by rapport and a man's charisma. When a woman feels she has a lot in common with a man she is far more tempted by him. And of course, if I can make her laugh, my chances of 'pulling' her increase tenfold.

Armed with as much knowledge about the girl as possible, I await a phone call from my client telling me where/when his partner is on a night out. I make sure I study her photo carefully so I get the right girl, and then I approach the situation in the same way I would if I were on a night out with the intention of 'pulling'. I begin with a cheeky smile, a witty comment or compliment, something to catch her attention. I then get chatting to my target, steering the conversation to those things we have in common. When girls are on a night out with friends they love being flattered by lots of attention.

Fortunately, I've always had a knack of making women feel good. Although I consider myself to be a good-looking guy, it's not all about looks. Ever since school, I realised that what appeals most to women is good conversation. They love to be complimented too. My easygoing and confident manner means that I've never found it difficult to attract the opposite sex. I'm a natural born flirt so I love the way I earn my money. It's a dream job really. Being paid to wine and dine beautiful, and sometimes not quite so beautiful, women beats being stuck in an office all day. In fact, it beats flying too. Of course, I have to try and keep myself in shape and looking good: a minger with a beer belly wouldn't get very far in my line of work, but I rely much more on charisma and a sense of humour.

After I've chatted up a woman it's up to her to make a move. Our entire conversation is recorded using hidden equipment, usually taped to my chest or stomach and the whole affair is videoed by a colleague strategically seated nearby. There are three things I look out for when engaged in conversation: if the target denies she is in a relationship, if she offers me her number, or if she leans in for a kiss – one or all of these things signal to me that she has fallen for the trap and I then make my excuses and leave.

This can be a tricky time. I have had occasions where the girl has reached the point where she wants to take things to the next level and is not at all happy to let me go without taking her there.

'Why won't you come back to mine?' one girl said, grabbing my crotch. I have to admit there have been times when I've been very tempted; what red-blooded male would want to turn down sex on a plate with a gorgeous girl?

I always hope, for the sake of the client, that the lady in question gives me the cold shoulder and if she does I'm a happy man. I get paid either way and my client will be thrilled and much relieved. It's not easy to be the bearer of bad news, but most people prefer to know the truth, however difficult or painful it might be to accept. I hand over the evidence and leave it to the client to decide whether his partner overstepped the mark and whether she can possibly be trusted.

While honeytrapping, I have found that women are less likely to be on the lookout for casual sex in the way men seem to be. Only 50 per cent of women fall for the honeytrap. While this figure may seem quite high, it is significantly lower than the number of men willing to cheat. Of course, there are a few less attractive girls who may be very much in love with their partner but who can't believe their luck when they get all the attention and compliments from a stranger. But generally those who fall for my charms are unhappy in their relationship, or not in love, or both.

Take one of my most recent targets, Lisa.

It's mid-April and I'm attempting to get my head around my tax return. It's one of my least favourite aspects of running my own business and, unlike most other times, I'm willing an urgent assignment to turn up and rescue me from the dreaded Inland Revenue.

As if on cue, the telephone rings. I should let the answer phone cut in, but I make a dive for it before I miss my reprieve.

'Hello, Expedite Detective Agency, Richard speaking.'

'Hi, it's Mikey... it's my wife, Lisa. She, I mean she's erm, I mean I...'

'You think you might need one of our services, Mikey? Tell me a little about the problem and I can explain how I think we might help.'

It's the same old story: men and their reluctance to admit to a problem. I find when women ring the office they launch into details of their situation, almost with a sense of relief at voicing their fears, but we men don't admit to perceived weakness or failure easily, and I find I have to drag it out of them when they call.

Mikey is no exception. In fact, he's even more reluctant than most to fill me in on the details. Twenty minutes later, and after many well-phrased searching questions, I find I'm dealing with a man who basically needs a honeytrap test on his wife.

Mikey and Lisa have been together for five years. They met while he was on a business trip in Sweden and have barely been apart since then. As far as Mikey is concerned, Lisa is the love of his life and everything about their relationship has, up until now, been a fairytale. It was his birthday when they first met. He was enjoying a few well-earned drinks with colleagues, and there she was sipping a glass of champagne and occasionally throwing flirtatious glances in his direction. After a few drinks, he plucked up the courage to talk to her, and she rather brazenly suggested he buy a bottle of champagne for the two of them, which he was more than happy to do. By the end of the business trip, they'd shared more than champagne and Mikey was anxious to meet up again back in London.

Mikey sounds pleased as he tells me Lisa wasn't all that keen to meet up at first, but he won her over by sending orchids, Bollinger champagne and pistachio chocolates to her office – all the things she'd told him she loved during their time together in Sweden. Eventually she agreed to a date in London, but only if he took her for a meal at the Oxo Tower Restaurant overlooking the Thames. Mikey loved that Lisa was so confident and so sure of what she wanted. He immediately booked a table, and their relationship went from there.

Two months ago, Mikey applied for a £20,000 overdraft and bought a Tiffany diamond engagement ring so he could ask for

Lisa's hand in marriage. He booked a table for the two of them, again at the Oxo Tower Restaurant, got down on one knee in front of all the other diners and proposed. She was delighted with the ring and agreed to be his wife.

So far, I'm thinking Mikey and Lisa's life sounds like something out of a magazine, but there are a few details that don't quite sound like the fairytale romance Mikey is painting, and of course if everything is as perfect as it sounds he wouldn't be on the phone to me. Maybe he's just an insecure man who wants to test out his partner before committing to marriage. But I think there's probably more to the story.

'Everything was brilliant after I proposed. Lisa was so happy with her ring, and I was so proud she'd agreed to marry me,' says Mikey. 'But when I told Edward earlier this week – that's my best friend – he didn't look happy. I said to him: "What's wrong? It's good news, isn't it?" He didn't say anything right away. He just sort of looked at the floor. But then he said, and I'll never forget this, he said: "She's cheating on you, mate." My mouth just hit the floor, you know. I couldn't believe what he was saying to me. I thought, maybe he's jealous, you know? He just doesn't want me to be happy. But deep down I knew Edward wouldn't make anything like that up.'

'How could he know that?' I ask. 'About Lisa?'

'He works with her,' Mikey says. 'He got a job in the same company last year. Anyway, I said, "Are you sure?" And he said he was pretty sure. He'd heard from this other guy who said... he said he slept with her last month. And Edward said she'd been seen kissing blokes when she went out for drinks with the girls.'

I can hear Mikey struggle to keep the emotion from his voice.

'I don't want it to be true, but it's all I can think about. What if she's not the person I think she is?'

I feel so bad for Mikey. A few days ago he was on top of the world – a young man with a beautiful fiancée and a wedding to look forward to. But now he's riddled with doubt: doubt about Lisa and doubt about himself. Is he capable of making the right choices about women?

'Lisa's got a work trip coming up this weekend,' Mikey tells me. 'A conference in Hertfordshire. I can't get the idea out of my head that she's going to cheat on me. I just can't bear the thought. It's been eating me up. I've got to know if she's who I thought she was.'

I get as many details as I can about Lisa, her work, her circle of friends and the conference this weekend. Then I explain to Mikey how it all works and what to expect: particularly, how he might feel if his suspicions are confirmed. I've had a few grown men shout, swear and cry on my shoulder when presented with evidence that their partner succumbed to my advances. For one man, seeing film footage of me chatting up his partner was too much to bear, and he swung for me. Fortunately, he calmed down quickly, apologised profusely and tried to pay double what he owed.

I wonder if Lisa is the sort of woman to break a man's heart – a woman who uses men for what she can get, and has no particular loyalty to her partner. Certainly, Mikey's story set some alarm bells ringing. It sounds like Lisa tests Mikey by asking for expensive meals and gifts – a sign that she isn't all that secure, and perhaps doesn't have much respect for him. What will happen if, at some point, he can't buy her the things she wants? Will she just move onto the next man? And if she's as money hungry as she sounds, I fear for Mikey's ability to pay for a lifestyle that meets her high standards. After all, he's already in £20,000 of debt and that's just for her engagement ring.

Later that week, I book myself into the Watermill Hotel in Hemel Hempstead, where Lisa will be attending an energy conservation conference with ten work colleagues. I'll be acting as a honeytrapper, as per Mikey's instructions, but I'll also be watching for flirtatious goings on between Lisa and other conference members. After all, there's no point wading in with my Mikey Bond charm, Martini at the ready, if I'm treading on the toes of someone Lisa already has feelings for.

I manage to book a room next to Lisa's, since Mikey has helpfully photocopied her conference pack, and I spend the week reading up on environmental policy and eco-friendly housing so I can wow Lisa with conversation at the bar. Or at the very least, send her into such a hypnotic state of boredom that she throws herself at me to shut me up.

It's Friday evening and I'm sat in every PI's second office: the hotel bar. I'm wearing a pressed, white shirt and tailored dinner jacket, but I've resisted the urge to order a vodka Martini, shaken not stirred. Instead, I sip a white coffee, accompanied by the obligatory caramel-coloured, plastic-wrapped biscuit, and wonder if Sean Connery ever stayed at a Best Western Hotel.

Lisa and her colleagues arrived around an hour ago, and are now at a table opposite enjoying a few Friday night drinks before the busy working weekend ahead. Lisa is a delicious chocolate box of a woman – she has everything any man could want: beautiful, with a gorgeous figure and intelligence into the bargain. She is a stunningly attractive woman, and every man at the table is captivated by her, as, I must admit, am I. It's not just her psychical appearance that's mesmerising, but the way she holds herself, moves her body around and smiles a big, intelligent, sexy smile whenever she's pleased by something, which is often. There is a pretty woman next to her wearing immaculate, well-tailored clothing, colour-coordinated accessories and a sleek, professional business hairstyle, but she seems invisible next to Lisa – and the downturned, sour expression on her face tells me she knows it.

I spend the evening watching Lisa, which is no hardship since I can hardly take my eyes off her. But nothing untoward happens, and I end up drinking coffee after coffee as I watch the group talk, laugh and drink well into the night. Lisa switches from white wine to sparkling mineral water as the night goes on, so she's still radiant and lively at quarter to midnight, even though some of her colleagues are a bit worse for wear.

At midnight the bar closes, and the group get up and make their way to their rooms. I head to my room too, and listen out for any noises that suggest Lisa is entertaining a guest next door. There are none, and within a few hours I hang up my dinner jacket and fall asleep.

It's 7.30 a.m. and I'm enjoying the hotel's complimentary breakfast while witnessing some truly hung-over individuals crawl into the dining room and force down dry toast and coffee with grim, green expressions.

The conference schedule pack tells me the group have seminars all day, finishing up with a Q&A session hosted by their company MD. I spend the day holed up in my hotel room with my laptop, with Planet Rock for company, catching up on reports for other clients and researching the latest gadgetry available to private sleuths. Late afternoon I make my way down to the hotel lounge and wait.

At 5.30 p.m. a group of tired, crumpled-looking individuals emerge from the conference room and trudge towards the dining area for their evening meal – which, the conference pack tells me, means more speeches. But at least there's a Saturday-night social planned for everyone in the hotel bar afterwards, complete with free drinks.

The good news is that tonight has all the ingredients that could tempt Lisa to be unfaithful: a few glasses of wine, a weekend away from 'real life' and the advances of yours truly. Well, perhaps not the last one – maybe a work colleague will do my job for me. We'll see.

After dinner, Lisa returns to her room to change so I head straight for the bar. An hour later, I'm beginning to worry that I've been stood up – and my date doesn't even know she's supposed to be meeting me. I order yet another orange juice and settle down for a long sit-in. There's no getting away from it: Lisa is a very attractive, intelligent woman and my usual cool, calm, charming persona has developed more than a few chinks. I'm eager for her to come down, if only to break the monotony. She is certainly lovely to watch. I down my drink in one, and the second I do Lisa walks into the bar, oozing style and sophistication in a figure-hugging, corseted black dress and subtle, diamond jewellery. She's flanked by two male work colleagues, and trailing behind is the woman who sat with them yesterday who, my keen people-reading skills tell me, is more than a little annoyed by the attention Lisa is getting, but is hiding it behind a sickly, fake smile.

At the bar, Lisa moves deliberately away from the two men and begins talking to the fake-smile woman. They're only a few feet away from me, and I can smell Lisa's perfume: expensive, elegant and alluring.

'Gosh! I'm so tired. Aren't you tired, Carol?' Lisa smiles at the woman. 'It's been such a long day.'

The woman, Carol, gives a humourless laugh.

'I don't get tired. I can work seven days a week if I need to.'

Lisa nods and smiles.

'Lucky you, I'm exhausted!' She tries to lay a friendly hand on Carol's arm, but Carol is quick to turn away.

'Edward!' Carol shouts. 'Edward, darling, how are you?'

Edward? A tall man with a chiselled face strides up to the bar; I wonder. Could it be... Mikey's friend Edward?

'What would Lisa like?' Edward calls back from the bar, and Carol's expression immediately hardens.

'Why don't you ask her?' She stalks off to a table.

Lisa is clearly uncomfortable with the exchange, and pulls out her purse.

'Don't anyone worry about me. I'm not sure what I want yet, anyway.'

The chance is there, so I take it. I scoop up a wine list from the bar and sidestep towards Lisa.

'I'd recommend the Sauvignon Blanc,' I say, giving her a friendly smile, 'if you like crisp wines. Are you more of a sweet or savoury kind of girl?' I grin cheekily, as if I know what a terrible line it is but can't help myself.

Lisa laughs loudly, and smiles warmly back.

'I'd like to think I'm sweet, but some people here would probably say I'm savoury. Or maybe she would prefer the comparison between sweet and sour,' she says, her eyes flickering towards Carol, then back to me. 'Oh, I don't mind really. Anything. If you say Sauvignon Blanc, that sounds good to me.'

She orders her drink, refuses my offer to pay for it and returns to her work colleagues. I wait a moment, then take a table near the group, with my back to them so they don't feel like I'm listening, but near enough to hear every word. As the minutes pass, the conversation between Carol and everyone else at the table becomes increasingly strained. It's clear that, at least in Carol's mind, she and Edward have some kind of relationship going on, but he's lavishing attention on Lisa.

'We all know you and your expensive tastes, Lisa!' Edward bellows suddenly, and everyone, Lisa included, bursts out laughing.

'It's not me!' Lisa insists. 'It's Mikey. He's the big spender. Honestly – this ring was his choice.'

'That's our Mikey,' says Edward. 'Splashing the cash. He was always a show-off.'

'No, honestly.' Lisa is adamant. 'He's not like that. He's just generous.' She sounds very proud as she says this, and I think what a lucky guy Mikey is. Having watched Lisa for the weekend, my original suspicions have completely dissolved and been replaced with new ones. I certainly don't think Lisa is only after Mikey for his money. That just doesn't seem to be who she is.

At 12 a.m. the hotel bar lights flash on and off and the group make their way upstairs to bed. I'm happy to join them: it's been a long evening, even though luckily I don't have a day of seminars to attend tomorrow.

I've barely closed my hotel door, when I hear a gentle knocking in the corridor. Slowly and ever so quietly, I open my door – just a fraction – and listen for what's going on outside. The knocking continues for a moment, then a door opens and I hear Edward's voice.

'Lisa. Please. Let me in.'

I hear a squeak as a door opens.

'Oh *Edward*.' It's Lisa's voice. 'Please. Stop embarrassing yourself. Go away.'

I try to memorise everything I'm hearing for Mikey's report. It's not evidence that can be used in court, but it's usually good enough for clients, who know as an objective third party I have no reason to make anything up.

I hear her push the door closed, but there's a clunk as something stops it – probably Edward's foot.

'Don't worry about Carol,' Edward slurs, in a voice that's far too loud for this time of night. 'It's been over for months. She just can't accept it. She was just one of those things that happened. It's always been you.'

'*Edward!*' Lisa's voice is an angry whisper. 'You're drunk. Leave me alone. I'm in love with your best friend. We're engaged! What's the matter with you?'

There's a noise that sounds like a throaty sob. I presume it must be Edward, because Lisa's voice is softer as she says:

'Come on, Edward. You're a good-looking guy. You could get loads of girls. Why me? You don't even know anything about me.

I could be a terrible kisser, for all you know.' She laughs, trying to lighten the mood.

'What's so great about Mikey, anyway?' Edward says. 'He's not even that good-looking. OK, he's Mr Moneybags, but so what? Just one night. Please. Just give me one…'

'Good night, Edward.' Lisa shuts the door with a bang, and after a moment I hear Edward sigh, then slope back along the corridor.

'So that's the good news,' I tell Mikey, who is sitting opposite me in a quiet corner of the local pub, an untouched pint of Stella in front of him. 'Lisa's a wonderful woman.'

'And the bad news?' Mikey leans forward, worry etched on his handsome, young face.

'Your friend Edward is a liar and a troublemaker and you're better off rid of him.' I drop the report on the table, and turn to the section about Edward – and his behaviour outside Lisa's hotel room. Mikey scans it quickly, a frown growing as he does so. When he's finished reading, he shakes his head in disbelief.

'After all I've done for him,' he says. 'I paid his credit card bill off last year. Did you know that? Five grand, because he came crying to me – I can't afford this, I can't afford that. He was so worried about what Carol would think of him.' He takes a sip of his pint. 'How can he live with himself? He knows Lisa's the best thing that ever happened to me. To try and ruin what we have…'

I nod, and let him rant and rave for a few minutes. He has a right to be angry, but when that anger subsides he'll count his blessings. He's discovered his fiancée is the faithful, good-hearted person he always thought she was, and from what I can see they'll have a long and happy life together. He's a lucky man.

3

SEX, LIES, THE PI AND HIS VIDEO CAMERA

I have dealt with hundreds of cases over the past ten years, and there is little doubt that most of them involve infidelity. Fear of being cheated on is a widespread emotion for most people in a relationship, and once a seed of insecurity has been sown sometimes the only way to achieve peace of mind is to be presented with hard evidence – jealous minds are satisfied by very little else. Often my clients have no idea whether their spouse or partner is up to no good or not, but have begun to notice a sudden change in behaviour: perhaps a few more sessions at the gym than usual, or a sudden and unexplained interest in fashion. Quite commonly, it's something subtle that sets alarm bells ringing, such as a partner volunteering information for no apparent reason or making small changes to their daily routine.

Clients worried about a partner's infidelity tend to approach me in a very sorry state, and I really feel for them. They hover on the verge of rejection and many tell me it's like living in a nightmare, falling prey to horrible thoughts, fantasies and insecurities. One lady said she felt as if she were falling into an abyss of lonely suffering – what man wouldn't want to help a woman in this kind of distress?

Employing a private detective to investigate suspected infidelity provides a one-way ticket to the truth, and I try to remind the client that once this route has been taken there is no going back. Often the worried partner has been concealing their doubts for a long time – months, sometimes even years – preferring to turn a blind eye rather than lose the person they love. In some situations, the 'ostrich method' is an effective way of dealing with the problem, as affairs do tend to burn out, but I think living like this takes its toll, knocking a person's confidence and draining them of energy. So when people find the strength to employ me and discover the truth, I do my best to listen sensitively and understand how courageous they are to make contact.

While honeytrapping accounts for a fair amount of my time, much of my work is focused on following cheating partners around on a motorbike, armed with a camera around my neck. The majority of my clients are women (and often wives of police or firemen – shift work offers ample opportunities to cheat and avoid the need for fictitious engagements) who have a suspicion that their partner is cheating on them, and one of the most amazing things I have witnessed since doing this job is a woman's intuition. If she thinks he is straying she is usually correct.

By the time a person feels the need to employ my services, they have usually already stored up more than enough doubts and suspicions and many feel they need to face the cold hard truth so that they can move on, however painful the facts may be. All the same, they are paying for information they would really prefer not to hear. I think the idea that their loved one might love another is most hurtful to them, as most people's biggest relationship fear is that they'll lose the love of their partner to someone else. I often witness the worst fears of my clients coming true.

I can think of only a handful of incidences where the woman has not been justified in suspecting her partner. One such case was a young wife whose suspicion was aroused when her husband left the house every Friday evening, reluctant to tell her where he was going. He seemed coy and secretive, so she employed me to follow him. It turns out he was visiting his mum and doing chores for her around the house and he didn't want his new wife to think of him as a 'mummy's boy'. Sadly, innocent explanations for suspicious behaviour are rare.

One of the hardest things I have to deal with is witnessing people's pain when I reveal their partner's infidelity. The fact is that no one likes to have the wool pulled over their eyes and no one enjoys being treated like a mug, and I try to remember that when I'm about to reveal to someone that their partner has betrayed them. I'm almost always armed with hard evidence, and I think in a way it helps clients, who have generally been feeling insecure and miserable for a long time, to see the facts in black and white. Indeed, clients are often eager for the facts so that they can be confident in dealing with the closure of their relationship. I think it helps them to move on. I am a big softie really and I find it difficult to watch their pain. However, once the unhappy deed is done I try to forget the hurt I've seen and do my best not to worry about the client once I've walked out the door.

I have had both men and women sobbing on my shoulder, but I try to remember that my job is to uncover the facts and then leave, moving on to the next job and leaving the client to deal with the aftermath. When a woman sobs on my shoulder I feel protective towards her and a little guilty, since I'm the one delivering the bad news she'd prefer not to hear. A number of times my female clients have gone so beyond rational thought that they respond to my comforting arm around their shoulder and try to take things further. I realise how vulnerable they are feeling and gently dissuade them. I'm not a bloke who could take advantage of a woman, however tempted I may feel. They are often devastated, their confidence is shattered and they are searching for some comfort and reprieve from the hurt they are feeling.

That's not to say that I've always managed to take the chivalrous line; there was one instance when I revealed the bad news of a cheating husband to a stunningly sexy French woman living in a huge house in a salubrious part of London. She received the news with dignity and remained calm, but I could see the hurt in her eyes. She buried her head in my chest for a comforting hug and as she gazed up at me with tears in her eyes I couldn't resist going in for a kiss. She responded instantly and soon we were kissing passionately. I left her then, but returned a couple of days later and what followed was a brief but passionate fling. I look back on that case with fondness and good memories.

I suppose I am affected by every case in one way or another as I can remember with clarity every single job that I've worked on, even back to 1999 when I was first paid to track a cheat. My client was a pregnant woman who was convinced that her husband, a businessman who owned a phone bureau, was playing away from home. For four nights I jumped on my motorbike and followed her husband in his car. He wasn't up to any mischief so I went back to my client and suggested that she stop. As it was the first job of this kind I had taken on I felt really bad taking money from a pregnant woman, but she insisted I carry on following her husband. She was paying for the surveillance out of his company's budget, so this helped appease my guilty feelings somewhat.

On the sixth night I caught him red-handed. I followed him to a local park where he met his lover, and I snapped a few shots of him kissing her intimately.

I broke the news to his pregnant wife and she had one more request: could I arrange for the woman to have an accident? I had to disappoint her, telling her that PIs investigate then leave – they don't get involved in the mess that's left behind.

Not everyone reacts to the news in the same way, but there seem to be four common reactions: disbelief (despite the hard evidence), anger, distress or total impassivity. Many do have violent thoughts of revenge, however, and indeed one woman recently asked me to return to her husband and 'kneecap' him. I had to tell her that my services don't stretch to that line of work. I am a private investigator, not Edward Woodward's *Equaliser*.

When I first started working as a private investigator, I thought clients might want to shoot the messenger when confronted with the bad news, but not a single one of them has reacted in that way. I think it may be because they can feel I sympathise with them. I try to be understanding and have usually built a rapport with them before I have to go in with the bad news.

The thing clients often find most difficult to accept is that when they have previously confronted their partner, there has been an insistence that nothing is going on. Many women are told they are neurotic and unreasonable, and worry they're going mad, so when they find out they were right all along it's not surprising some of them feel the need for revenge. Presenting the cheating partner with the damning evidence can be empowering for them. Often, for a long time the client has felt helpless and in the dark, so handing over the photographs to their cheating husband can feel like a victory: a miserable one, but a victory nonetheless.

When the size of future maintenance payments and possible forced sale of the family home can be affected by the strength of a client's case, there is an awful lot at stake. Add custody of the children into the mix and you have an explosive cocktail. It is critical to gather as much hard evidence as possible in order to settle the case in the client's favour, so if a client tells me she's found an unexplained thong stuffed under the back seat of her beloved hubby's car (this has happened so many times I'm tempted to write a book on how to catch a cheat and list 'search for alien panties under the back seat of husband's car' as one of the top ten methods), my advice to secure the offending item in an evidence bag along with her hubby's DNA may be enough to secure a sizable settlement.

Some time ago it was unusual for anyone but the affluent to employ the services of a PI for divorce cases, but nowadays we're used across the classes. Private eyes are still regularly used by the affluent, however, since they have a whole lot more to lose, and I have worked for a large number of prominent people, including MPs, celebrities and a number of footballers' WAGs too. According to Grant Thornton financial advisers, in 2006 nearly half of all wealthy divorcing couples in the UK engaged the services of a PI to confirm or rebut allegations of infidelity. The figure for 2005 was just 18 per cent, and this comes as no surprise to me – the growth in this type of business has been palpable and business is booming. Although it hasn't been necessary to prove adultery to obtain a divorce since the 1960s, people these days are generally savvier about how divorce proceedings can be swung in their favour, and a wife often achieves a bigger settlement if she can prove betrayal.

High-profile cases, such as Ingrid Tarrant's use of a private detective to confirm her intuition about Chris, have brought attention to the work I do and increased its popularity. Ingrid hired a private detective to follow her husband over several weeks, before filing for divorce in September 2006 based on the evidence she was given. Although it took eighteen months of wrangling, the hard evidence of his infidelity secured her half of his £25 million fortune in their divorce settlement. The American banking heir Matthew Mellon was put on trial in 2007, accused of asking a detective agency to hack into the computer of his former wife, Tamara Mellon, the founder of the Jimmy Choo shoe empire. He denied the charge of conspiring to cause unauthorised modification of computer material and was found not guilty, but it is said that companies offering a computer hacking service boast a large number of high-profile clients.

I aim to catch the cheat, either by photograph or video footage, on at least three separate occasions. Sometimes I am hired to cover special events, such as office parties or social events, when a client is concerned that their partner's behaviour may get out of hand. As I write this, just last week I was contacted by an intelligent, married lady in her early forties who requested I follow her husband to a work party and report back on his activities. She'd become suspicious as for the first time ever her husband had purchased new underwear and started shaving every morning without fail.

A few moments of observing her husband on his way to work told me he was an uncoordinated and unobservant sort of man who put so much concentration into moving one foot in front of the other that he was unlikely to notice being followed. As it turns out, he was both unobservant and indiscreet. He left work that evening arm-in-arm with a young woman who worked in his office, and within moments they'd climbed into his Volvo and were kissing passionately. Twenty minutes later, they entered an anonymous-looking city hotel – a narrow, Georgian building squashed between a sandwich shop and a dry cleaners – and had their own private party inside for over three hours. When I told his wife, she wasn't sure what she was most upset about: her husband's infidelity or the fact he wore clean boxers when he treated this woman to a night of passion.

There are a myriad of gadgets available to spy on partners: trackers that can be fixed to the underside of cars by magnet, software that can record every keystroke tapped into a computer keyboard and even a device that can retrieve deleted text messages. There can be no hiding place for someone who has a partner determined to find out the truth.

I have only ever been caught out twice: once, when a husband realised his car had a tracking device on it, then went through his wife's handbag and found my business card, and a second time when my target spotted me following him. He went home and quizzed his wife and she confessed that she had employed me.

I have to make sure I keep my wits about me and I never take anything at face value. I've learnt so often that true facts don't always reveal themselves without a little digging, particularly in cases of infidelity. Love and sex make an explosive cocktail and with a dose of jealousy thrown in the combination can become lethal. Of all the cases I deal with, those involving spurned or cheated lovers require the most delicate and sensitive handling.

It's 6 p.m. on Thursday night, and I'm updating my weekly expenses when the phone rings. It still excites me when I get a call, even though half the time it's someone trying to sell me insurance or asking if I have any junior vacancies. Having said that, tonight I was hoping to make it out of the door before 7 p.m. and down a relaxing pint in the local boozer.

I pick up the phone. 'Hello?'

'Uh... Hello. I don't know... I wondered if...' There's a long pause. 'Perhaps you could help me with my wife?' It's a man, and he sounds breathless and extremely anxious. The few men that do manage to swallow their pride and ask for my help usually are.

'How can I help, exactly?'

I hear sobbing down the phone – big, gasping sobs that finish with loud nose blowing and a large intake of breath.

'She's... seeing another man.' He takes a few more breaths, and sounds calmer. 'My wife... it's a man from work. I think she's seeing a man from work. Richard. She says she's going away this weekend for a...' Sobbing threatens to take over him again, but he manages to keep it together. '...girls weekend. She says she and the girls have a weekend planned; a spa treat. But I think girls will be the last thing on her mind.'

We talk a little more, and he tells me his name is Alan, and he wants his wife followed for the whole weekend. I get the impression it makes the agony of her suspected affair more bearable if he has some kind of knowledge, and perhaps therefore control, of the situation.

I ask that he wire an advance straight into my business account to cover initial expenses: a procedure I usually follow, since these kinds of weekends can swallow up a large amount of ready cash. He tells me this will be difficult as he has to fly off to Amsterdam early the following morning and this is the reason he can't follow his wife himself. I agree, against my better judgement, to sort out expenses and my fee on his return and start to pack for a wintry mini-break, hopefully in the UK. It wouldn't be the first time I've packed up ready to follow an amorous cheating spouse on a UK break, only to find they head for the nearest airport, and then of course I have to abort the mission and pass the news to my anxiously waiting client. Apparently Alan's wife, Caroline, is extremely organised, so Alan is confident that if she were off on a foreign trip he would know about it. We'll see.

I have to admit I love this part of my job. Some of my less impulsive counterparts would rather sit in the office conducting research from their desk, but I love to get stuck in and go wherever the case takes me. I pack a few books to take with me (I always have a couple on the go to suit whichever mood I'm in at the time), and of course my usual equipment – binoculars, video surveillance equipment, zoom-lens camera – and a dapper suit, since I'm not sure how upmarket the destination will be. If the gentleman in question is trying hard to impress his lady it may be fairly swanky. Caroline's husband had no idea of her destination, so I make sure I fill up with petrol, as the last thing I need is to lose them after travelling 200 miles while I stop at a garage.

At 5.30 a.m. the next day, I'm waiting outside Alan and Caroline's house. Alan is confident she won't leave before him and I arrive just in time to see him pull out of the end of the road. He gives me what I'm sure he believes to be a casual glance, but anyone with half a trained eye would catch the look of sly recognition on his face. During our phone conversation earlier today, he told me he would love to do my job, but I think he's best suited to his occupation as a senior accounts manager, and shouldn't apply to the secret service in a hurry.

I wait. A few groups of children clip-clop down the street on their way to school, chattering loudly, their rucksacks slipping around on their shoulders. They look like they're enjoying their freedom before the school gates open and I envy their ability to move around and do as they like. An annoying aspect of surveillance is the need for absolute concentration when tracking a target, and as the hours pass I long to pick up a book, crossword or anything to alleviate the boredom. But it only takes a minute for someone to leave their house, jump in a car and be gone, so constant vigilance is always needed.

I generally park some distance from the target so as to avoid becoming an object of interest to them. Most people unconsciously become aware of the usual cars that occupy their own road and they may notice something a little out of the ordinary. The last thing I want is to bring attention to myself.

As the second hour of surveillance approaches I'm beginning to lose enthusiasm. I sit in complete silence, checking and rechecking my camera and other equipment. Stillness becomes oppressive in the confined space of my car. I long to whistle or switch the radio to Planet Rock – anything to break the unnatural silence.

I check my camera for the fifty-first time and catch movement in my peripheral vision: a dark blue Audi convertible pulls into the substantial driveway of number 14 and within seconds the door opens and Caroline rushes over, leans into the driver's window and greets her lover with a kiss lasting over thirty seconds. I take a few shots and make the most of the ample opportunity to capture the moment. Sometimes I have to be quick off the mark to catch a lover's kiss, but not this time.

Dressed in a pretty dapper pinstripe suit and shiny shoes, her lover takes her suitcase and holdall to the car and, rather chivalrously, opens the passenger door for her. It's a pleasant, loving gesture and one I don't usually see between two people carrying out a covert affair. Usually it's all quick explosions of passion when it's assumed no one's watching, and fidgety, sideways glances when it's assumed somebody is.

I take another shot of them kissing, then check the digital screen to make sure the pictures are in focus. They are, and I have to admit they look good together: an attractive pair. I guess Alan will be pretty gutted when he sees the pictures. This couple are very much into each other – you don't have to be a professional to see that.

As the Audi pulls out of the driveway I prepare myself for a nightmare journey. Setting off during rush hour on a Friday afternoon before a Bank Holiday weekend is not my idea of good planning, but in my job you don't get to choose journey times. One of the most annoying factors in following a loved-up couple on a dirty weekend is the lack of control I have over any of the travel arrangements; I have to leave when they do and obviously take the same route too.

Four and a half hours later we arrive at our destination: a country manor hotel in the Lake District. It's a beautiful, old building with bright-green ivy running over its white walls and I must concede a good choice for a romantic break – the sort of place you could hole up in and not leave for a few days.

I allow them some time to check in, and then telephone the hotel from my car to make sure they have a single room available. Last time I followed a couple to a hotel, I had to stay in the car as everything was fully booked – not very salubrious, but at least they only stayed overnight and I captured enough evidence of adultery to satisfy even the most querulous judge in that short time.

As I watch them come back out into the car park for their luggage, I get a sinking feeling. There's a lot more coming out of the boot than the suitcase and holdall I saw Caroline pack earlier today. A massive, hard-plastic case with wheels and a long handle has just been unloaded, followed by two huge sports bags and two more leather holdalls. It looks like the couple have either planned a mountain expedition for the weekend, or are staying much longer than a couple of days. I set off with a half-empty small suitcase, since my brief was that the couple would only be away for the weekend, but amid their sea of luggage my clean shirt, travel toiletries and two pairs of clean boxers feel a little inadequate.

The couple head back into the hotel, and I start getting my equipment ready for a long weekend.

It's 4.30 p.m. on Bank Holiday Monday, and it has indeed been a long weekend, but a very fruitful one. I've got a whole load of damning footage and am enjoying a black coffee in the hotel lounge while recording Caroline and her companion, Richard, enjoy a bottle of wine at the table opposite. I'm posing as a business guest, so I have my laptop and mobile phone set out in front of me while I discreetly observe the couple watch the sun set over the picture-perfect rolling hills.

It's becoming increasingly clear my sinking feeling was spot on. Even though it's the end of the weekend, this couple look like they're getting more comfortable, not ready to leave. And there's something else amiss too. Far from the usual furtive kisses and quiet conversation typical of a couple on an adulterous fling, these two are relaxed and comfortable, enjoying each other's company and talking without a care for who's listening. They're a happy pair, and I'm beginning to feel extremely sorry for my client.

I finished my last novel yesterday, so I was hoping to be back on the road by tomorrow, but as I watch the couple flick through a local walking guide and eagerly point at pictures I realise this is highly unlikely. Maybe they've got so caught up in each other they've lost track of the days, but I think it's much more likely this trip has been planned for more than a weekend from the start, which begs the question: Why did Caroline tell her husband it would just be for a day or two? It would make more sense to invent a story that covered the whole time she was with Richard, otherwise neighbours or friends might comment on her absence to Alan. I'm beginning to feel everything might not be quite as it seems with this case.

Two days later, I'm still in the Lake District hoping that today will be the day the couple decide to head home – for the sake of my client's wallet, if nothing else. I'm actually quite surprised the couple haven't moved to a cheaper place during this past week. In my experience, guilty people usually move around and I had hoped the pair might book themselves into a motel for the latter part of the week. But they remain blissfully settled in their £270 per night room and I remain comfortable, but restless, in a single room along the corridor.

'Your bill, sir.' A handsome waiter sets down my breakfast receipt, printed on thick paper and folded to fit the bone china saucer underneath it. After a quick glance at the total, I decide enough is enough. I pick up my mobile and ring Alan, sinking back into the high-backed lounge armchair to muffle my conversation.

'I'm still at the hotel, and I'm worrying for your bill,' I tell him. I'm relieved when he tells me he's just arrived back in the UK – answering this call on his mobile in Amsterdam wouldn't help his finances.

'Don't worry, don't worry,' he tells me. 'I just want you to watch her no matter what she does. And him. Watch them both and keep recording everything.'

I don't know if he's just not at all concerned with money, or whether monitoring his wife's affair is becoming something of an obsession.

'Do they look in love?'

A sadness has crept into his voice.

I take a sideways glance, and see the pair laughing in perfect unison, both their heads bobbing at the same time and their eyes meeting like long-lost friends. I've dined every evening on a table directly across from them for six days now, and it's been many months, years even, since I've seen a couple that look so well suited.

'Yes,' I tell him. 'Yes, they do.'

There's a long pause.

'Just stay as long as they stay. Keep recording and taking pictures. I'll pay whatever your expenses are.'

'OK, but I should warn you, Alan, they're not staying in a Holiday Inn. The bill is into the thousands already.' Even breakfasts of bacon and eggs in this kind of establishment don't come cheap.

'I don't care,' Alan tells me. 'Just stay. You leave when she leaves.'

'I'm sorry, Alan, I can't stay here indefinitely,' I tell him. 'I might need to be back in London any day now.' I had a phone call yesterday from a long-standing client, Gerald, who may need me urgently this week.

Alan seems to accept the fact observation can't go on forever, so I hang up and finish my breakfast. I'm happy to be wearing a clean shirt and underwear today as I tuck into my free-range eggs and organic bacon, but the new clothing is another expense I've had to put poor Alan's way. I was tired of washing clothes in the sink every evening and decided to splash out on a pack of seven boxers from Primark and a couple of reasonably priced shirts – striking a balance between not looking conspicuous in a top-class hotel and bearing in mind that the client would be footing the bill.

I've just finished my delicious scrambled eggs, when my mobile rings. It's Gerald.

'I need you to watch my wife tonight,' he says, before I've even had a chance to say hello.

I've been following his wife, Julie, on and off for around a year, as Gerald is convinced she'll be unfaithful as soon as his back is turned. When I first started tailing her, there was no evidence of infidelity – she would just leave the house in a dowdy outfit then arrive at her friend's place, where she would change into miniskirt, high heels and low-cut top, before going on to a club. It seemed more a case of a woman breaking free of her jealous husband than a cheating spouse.

However, recently she's been getting close to a young stockbroker who hangs around the nightclubs, and my observations suggest that if there isn't already something going on there soon will be. I can't help feeling that my client's mistrust of his wife is partly responsible – people with jealous partners sometimes end up rebelling by doing exactly what is expected of them all along.

Gerald tells me his wife says she's staying overnight at a girlfriend's house tonight, which is something that has never happened before, and he suspects she might be about to consummate her relationship with the young stockbroker. He's desperate to have her watched, and I agree immediately.

'OK,' I say, and hunt around for my notepad. 'I'll need to take a few details.'

He tells me his wife is supposedly heading to her friend Carla's house after work, who's just had a baby and needs some support during the evenings, but Gerald checked Julie's bag this morning and the obligatory sexy outfit lay amid her lipsticks and magazines. She's even added some spare underwear this time, and Gerald is going out of his mind with jealousy.

I head back to my room and start packing my things, deciding not to worry about leaving Caroline and Richard unobserved for the remainder of their trip. I have ample evidence of adultery and after six days all the footage is becoming very samey. Really, I'm doing Alan a favour by cutting short the spiralling expenses bill and leaving the happy couple to their holiday. There's little doubt in my mind that Alan and Caroline's relationship is in tatters, and the most important thing now is to convince him it's time to let go.

I drive back to London, and spend the early afternoon in my office finishing a comprehensive report for Alan and creating copies of all the camera shots and video footage. I let Alan know I'm back, and he asks to come meet me at my office to look over everything. Usually, I bring evidence to my client's homes, but since he's so keen to see it as soon as possible I agree, and within half an hour he's in my office reading the report and looking over all the photos and film footage.

I feel very sorry for him as he examines the evidence, as I can see the pain in his face and it's not in response to the astronomical expenses bill. He tells me he still loves Caroline dearly, but is very grateful that I've provided him with proof of his suspicions. He even compliments my professionalism. There's only one snag: he can't settle the bill for my services. Now he tells me! Congenial as ever, I assure him I can wait a little while for settlement. I may have a living to make, but I can appreciate the pressure he's under.

By the time Alan leaves, it's nearly 4 p.m. I jump in my car and head straight to Julie's place of work: an upmarket nail bar in Guildford, Surrey. I've spent many an evening watching her tidying nail polish bottles, wiping manicure tables and chatting away to the other girls in the shop before she leaves for the evening and heads out for a scantily dressed night on the town with her friends. Even in her clinical, manicurist's uniform it's clear she's a bubbly and fun-loving character and I've always found it sad that she feels the need to hide this from her husband.

As I watch her leave the shop and walk down the busy street, I think that for once her husband's suspicions may be well founded. She's nervous as a mouse, jumping as cars zoom past and constantly checking her mobile phone. At the end of the street, a silver Aston Martin DB9 pulls over and she nearly jumps out of her skin. It's lover boy: the young stockbroker she's been getting to know over the past few months, and she gives the street a good look up and down before diving into the passenger seat and throwing on a pair of huge Gucci sunglasses. The car speeds off and I run to my motorbike, parked a road away. Rush hour traffic and my knowledge of a few quiet side streets means I catch up with them quickly, but before long they pull over into the local train station car park and head inside towards the ticket counter.

I'm just quick enough to get into the station and overhear where they're buying tickets for: Manchester. Fortunately, Gerald has already wired an advance sum to deal with expenses, so despite Alan's delayed payment I have funds for a ticket and a meal onboard the train. I mentally thank Gerald for his early payments. However much a PI wants to help his clients, few can afford to work for the love of it and sometimes every penny counts.

We all head towards the platform, and I snatch an abandoned newspaper from a bench on the way. Clichéd as it sounds, papers are good props for concealing my face, and making sure my tail doesn't get too familiar with it. The train pulls in and we all get on.

Four hours later we arrive in Manchester, and I watch the couple enter a swanky hotel. Julie really seems to have fallen for this guy but, unlike the couple I've just left, the feeling doesn't seem to be mutual. Mr Stockbroker looks like something of a cad, and although he's clearly happy to have a beautiful woman on his arm he still has something of a wandering eye. He takes such a long look at two pretty girls walking past the hotel doorway I'm surprised Julie doesn't turn around and run back to the train station, but she seems too nervous to notice.

Now to make the difficult call to my client to fill him in on what's happening – and check he's OK to wire funds to my bank account for an overnight hotel stay.

The telephone conversation is every bit as hard as I imagined, and although Gerald is keen for me to continue observing his wife, he's absolutely devastated. Driven to despair by thoughts of Julie, whom he adores, spending the night with someone else, he asks me to dress as a room-service attendant, hide in the room and report back to him his wife's every move and exactly what she allows her lover to do. I have to draw the line now and again and this is one mission I refuse, but I agree to stay the night and provide him with photographic evidence of the couple leaving the following morning.

The next day, it's almost too easy to get pictures as Julie and the stockbroker leave the hotel room with their arms wrapped around each other, and even kiss passionately in the hotel foyer for good measure. I take the train back, drive straight over to see Gerald and show him the pictures. He looks at them with stoic acceptance, but when I explain that the guy seems somewhat of a ladies' man, Gerald has an idea. He still loves his wife, and asks me to arrange a honeytrap for the stockbroker so he can discredit Julie's lover and hopefully put an end to the affair. I feel a little hesitant about this course of action and not at all confident it will pay off, but Gerald is quite insistent so I agree. If I'm honest, I'm quite touched that he's so forgiving of his wife's adultery and still keen to win her back. I set the wheels in motion and arrange for a beautiful young woman to chat up the stockbroker and lure him on a date.

A few weeks later, I have the pleasure of telling Gerald that the honeytrap worked a treat, and the young stockbroker fell for our mystery brunette hook, line and sinker. I email him photos and my report, and he plans to take his wife out that very day for a private lunch, during which he'll show her evidence of exactly the sort of man she's carrying on with.

'I sent your final payment a week ago,' says Gerald, 'so we should be right up to date.'

Which reminds me: I still haven't had any word or payment from Alan.

I thank Gerald, and as soon as he hangs up I call Alan. But I can't get through. His line connects directly to a softly spoken lady announcing over and over again that the number is no longer in use.

Since Alan only gave me a mobile number, I really have no choice but to visit his home address, which is something I'm loath to do. I don't know whether he's told his wife about hiring a detective, so turning up unannounced might cause her to ask a lot of questions, but I don't see that I have much choice.

Within an hour I pull up on Alan's street, but now his wife's questions are the least of my worries. The house is clearly standing empty, and there are boards on the windows. It looks like Alan's done a runner.

I knock on a neighbour's door, and a young woman answers with a baby in her arms.

'Do you know what happened to the couple next door?' I ask. 'I'm a friend of theirs.'

'Oh, they moved,' the woman tells me. 'A few weeks ago.'

'Did you know Alan?' I ask.

'Alan?' She looks surprised. 'Yes, I've heard all about Alan. Caroline and I were good friends.'

It strikes me as a very strange thing to say, but since she seems quite open to chatting about the couple I ask: 'Are they still together? Caroline and Alan?'

'No, of course not,' she says, jiggling her baby up and down. 'That was over months ago. He's out of the picture, and Caroline and Richard are making a real go of their marriage. They decided to sell up the old house and start afresh somewhere new.'

I thank her for her help and head towards my car, my thoughts in turmoil. So the lovely Caroline was never my client's wife at all, but his mistress. And now she's been wooed back by her estranged husband, who decided to whisk her away to the Lake District in an attempt to repair the relationship that had presumably been damaged by my client. Truth really is stranger than fiction.

Something tells me Alan never intended to pay for my services, and that I'll be lucky if I see a penny for my trip away. I shake my head, disappointed in myself. I've been in this game long enough, I should be able to spot a shyster from a mile away, and I know better than to go on an expensive trip without claiming expenses first.

My thoughts turn to Gerald, my honest, paying client who always wires me money in advance. He must have shown his wife the honeytrap evidence by now, and I'm eager to know whether he's persuaded the love of his life to abandon her new flame and make a go of her marriage.

I dial his number on my mobile, and he answers on the first ring.

'It worked,' he says, before I have to ask. 'She's got rid of him and we're working at our marriage. I think we've got a good chance.'

'That's terrific,' I tell him. 'Truly, I'm very happy for both of you.'

Great news. Suddenly everything seems better – even if I've just paid for an expensive solo trip to the Lake District out of my own money. It's cases like Gerald's that reassure me I can be an ambassador for love and faithful marriage. I do sometimes feel responsible for causing pain to people, but I hope that in the long term I have helped them to make informed choices in their lives. And no matter how many 'Alans' I meet, I still intend to be honest and understanding with my clients, and endeavour to help them lead happier lives. I always remember what Friedrich Nietzsche wrote: 'He who gazes into the abyss should be careful, for the abyss will gaze back. He who hunts monsters should be wary that he does not also become a monster.'

4

ALL IS NOT WHAT IT SEEMS

As I mentioned in the introduction to this book, my world sometimes involves the investigation of events that most people find unpalatable to say the least, the sort of events not generally discussed in decent company. Nevertheless, however unfortunate, these events form a very real part of life and in my role as PI I sometimes find myself right at the sharp end. The following case involves almost every aspect of the underworld: drugs, gangs, bullying, dirty old men and a protection racket thrown in for good measure. Since the details are very personal I was reluctant to disclose them in a book but after a discussion with my client I was persuaded that it may help to warn others of what can happen when a vulnerable person is manipulated by the unscrupulous.

The case begins on Saturday night. It's been a long week and I could murder a curry. I've just finished a forty-eight-hour stakeout and I'm famished, fed-up and more than happy to spend a night in watching an England World Cup qualifier against Germany with some ex-colleagues, who just so happen to be due round any minute. I've already ordered enough tandoori chicken, lamb tikka, chicken vindaloo and naan bread to feed an entire football team, so no matter how abysmally England perform I know at least the boys and I will be well fed.

Unfortunately, the stakeout was a dead loss. I tailed a company director suspected of industrial foul play, but in forty-eight hours he did nothing dirtier than clean bird droppings from his car windscreen and I spent two muggy days stuck in my car watching everyone else enjoy the sunshine. Still, at least I've got a night with my old RAF mates to look forward to.

The lads bang on the door just as the takeaway arrives, and before long we're all sat in front of the TV eating curry so hot I think our forks might dissolve. Just as David Beckham wins the toss and heads to the wing ready for the forwards to kick-off, my mobile phone rings. Talk about bad timing.

'Hello, can I help you?'

It's not a number I recognise, but I promised a long-standing female client of mine that I would be available over the next few days if she had any more serious concerns over her teenage son and his alcohol-fuelled nights on the town. Maybe it's her, and she needs me to watch him for the evening. Praying it's my gas provider offering me a cheaper tariff, or even Mrs Banfield, the old eccentric of South Kensington in need of a chat, I answer while keeping the match in my peripheral vision.

The anxious tone in the female voice at the other end of the phone soon drags my concentration away from the dulcet tones of John Motson.

'My name is Mrs Noble,' she tells me. 'Our daughter has started stealing from us, and we're worried sick.'

Mrs Noble is a very well-spoken lady and I find myself subconsciously adjusting my accent to match hers, which causes Jimbo and the others to stare at me, amusement spreading across their faces. I decide the best thing to do is leave the room before they start taking the piss, which wouldn't be the most professional way to introduce a client to my agency. I don't want Mrs Noble to think we're a bunch of schoolboys.

'I understand your concerns, Mrs Noble. I'd be happy to try and help you. Shall I give you a call in the morning and I can take all the details then?'

I can hear the disappointment in her voice as she politely tells me this would be *'fine'*. I know women and their use of the word *fine*. In my experience, it usually means it's not fine at all.

'Of course I could pop over to see you now and take a full history of the problem if you'd prefer?'

'Oh yes please, Mr Martinez, thank you so much, that's wonderful, I'll give you our address.'

I take down the details of a wealthy area in Surrey called Kingswood, known locally as footballers' paradise. Within a few minutes I'm heading out the door, leaving the boys to their curry. They don't seem too bothered by my departure and I can't say I'm surprised. After all, they have everything they need for a perfect boys' night in, save a saucy stripper popping in at midnight. Rather reluctantly, resentfully even, I trudge down the path and head for Kingswood. As I reach Lower Kingswood the scenery changes and begins to get leafier. Even as dusk descends I can tell I'm driving into a rather pleasant neck of the woods. As Lower Kingswood becomes Kingswood, the houses seem to grow and the roads get wider, many of them marked PRIVATE on rather grand white signs on either side of the gated roads. I make out Woodland Drive and keep my eyes peeled for a house named 'Hawthorns'. I reach the end of the road without success and do a U-turn, cursing the local residents as I do so. Quite clearly money is no object in this part of the world, so why the bloody hell don't they light the signs of the house names? I continue to rant silently as I scour the houses and acknowledge I'm far more resentful than I should be at missing the match. Why was I so eager to answer the phone?

Finally I spot Hawthorns and overshoot the driveway by a few yards. I reverse and as I do I study the huge house, partially hidden by black iron gates about three metres high. It presents a majestic face to the road; I count at least six windows across the first floor, and the house appears to be as deep as it is wide. I press the buzzer on the intercom at the side of the gates and announce my name to the female voice floating eerily in the night air. The gates swing open smoothly, and I edge slowly forward.

The sound of my tyres on the shingle raises my mood a little: it's one of the sounds I love, besides the blissful clunk of leather on willow or the gentle gurgle of wine as it's first poured from bottle to glass.

Mrs Noble greets me at the huge oak doorway and I follow her into a large, open entrance hall with black marble flooring and thick white pillars. I'm a little taken aback by the warmth of her greeting and her easy manner. From our brief telephone call I'd managed to conjure an image of Helen Mirren in her movie portrayal of the queen, but Mrs Noble appears to be a warm, friendly person and my earlier resentment fades completely as I follow her through the entrance hall, a showplace for antiques and art, and into a huge library where I take a seat in the easy chair by the log fire. On the wall above the fire a huge mirror stands on the mantelpiece and the wall beyond features a life-size portrait of a semi-naked, large-boned woman, half-reclining on a chaise longue. Mrs Noble sits opposite and shows me a photograph of her daughter, Catherine. I see a shy, smiling girl with ears that stick out ever so slightly through her long, shiny dark hair. She looks healthy and well cared for.

It seems the problems began almost a year ago, just after Catherine's sixteenth birthday. Until then, Catherine had been a fun-loving, happy and carefree young girl, as she appeared to be in the photograph resting beside me on the arm of the sumptuous armchair; and an A-grade student into the bargain.

'At first I thought it might be hormone problems,' Mrs Noble explains. 'She was moodier than I'd ever known her before, and she started spending most of her evenings in her room. We've always been close and enjoyed each other's company, but it felt like all of a sudden she wanted to avoid me.'

Sounds like the usual teenage story I get from so many parents. Sometimes I think modern society is breeding a race of hermits. It does sound as though there have been sudden changes in Catherine's behaviour, however, and this in itself sets my alarm bells ringing. I get the impression that Mrs Noble has called me here this evening out of desperation, not knowing what else to do.

'Whenever I try talking to her she just snaps at me and strops off to her room, but that's not the worst of it. All those hours confined to her bedroom worried me, but now she's out all hours of the night, goodness knows where and she's skipping lessons at school. Yesterday was the final straw, when I finally confirmed what I've been suspecting for a few weeks now: Catherine is stealing from us.'

Mrs Noble's voice cracks and tears roll down her cheeks as she confesses this final humiliation. From my experience, this is often the point at which families struggle to hold it together, when they realise their child has sunk low enough to steal from his or her own loved ones. I imagine Catherine must have a pretty potent reason to take such drastic measures to get her hands on fast money.

'I don't want to cause you even more concern, Mrs Noble, but have you considered that Catherine may be taking drugs?'

'Yes, that's what terrifies me the most. That's why I need you, Mr Martinez. I need to find out what's going on with my daughter so I can help her before it's too late. I'm sure she's lying to us, and I need to know the truth.'

The truth. So many of my investigations involve finding out the truth for my clients, or to put it another way – uncovering the lies.

Mrs Noble dabs her eyes with a hanky as a plump middle-aged lady enters the library with tea served on a tray. All thoughts of the England match are now far from my mind: I'm hooked. I like Mrs Noble and I want to help her and her daughter. I sink further back into the deep leather chair and sip scalding hot tea while taking notes; I need a full history if I'm to identify the trigger causing so many traumatic changes in her daughter's life. I suggest tracking her daughter for a couple of days to see what she's getting up to when she should be at school, but Mrs Noble is convinced the best way to deal with the problem is confront Catherine directly. She feels if she can get her daughter to admit that she is stealing from her family she'll start to open up and reveal what's troubling her. In short, she wants me to carry out a lie detector test.

Throughout history, human beings have been obsessed with finding ways to discover if another person is lying. The following extract from a papyrus written by Vedas at around 900 BC instructs members of the society about how to root out liars involved in poisoning: 'A person who gives poison may be recognised. He does not answer questions, or they are evasive answers; he speaks nonsense, rubs the great toe along the ground and shivers; his face is discoloured; he rubs the roots of the hair with his fingers and he tries by every means to leave the house' (Paul V. Trovillo, 'A History of Lie Detection', *American Journal of Police Science*, vol. 29, 1939).

As well as having a dry mouth, the ancients also identified an increased pulse rate as identifying deceit. The Greek physician Erasistratus (300–250 BC) felt the pulse of the accused; an increased rate signalled confirmation of a lie. Lancisi in 1728 remarked: 'Emotion may be produced through the close dependence of mental functions upon the nerves, ganglia and coronary vessels of the heart.'

It's becoming increasingly common for clients to contact me and ask for tests to be carried out on their partners, but I have to say

Mrs Noble's request is a first. I've never yet been required to test someone's child. Lie detector tests, or polygraph tests, are used extensively in the US, where over a million tests are conducted every year for job-applicant screening and security vetting, to detect possible security or employment risks. Civil liberties organisations and trade unions are strongly opposed to their use, but in spite of this the polygraph remains very much a part of American society.

Use of the polygraph can be dangerous; it is a fallible procedure and hence it cannot be used as evidence before a court in the UK. It is possible to school yourself to pass a lie detector test, the simplest way being to step up your responses to the neutral questions by biting your tongue. The polygraph will then record little difference in reaction to the key and neutral questions.

Essentially, all that can be identified by the test is increased arousal. Confirmation of a lie cannot be identified 100 per cent accurately by the test. What can be determined are changes in breathing and blood pressure under emotional arousal. Underlying the emotional arousal could be a number of triggers, and whether those triggers are guilt, anger, embarrassment or fear cannot be discerned. Fear of being found out when guilty or fear of being implicated despite being innocent cannot be distinguished by a machine either.

In the UK, the Royal Commission on Criminal Procedure uphold the present ban on the use of polygraph tests as criminal evidence, since 'the test cannot confirm to the usual interpretation of beyond reasonable doubt'. As a result, polygraph tests are generally only used in the UK by private PIs at the request of clients. Having said that, the Ministry of Justice recently announced some sex offenders will be forced to take lie detector tests to see if they are still a danger to the public. The pilot scheme was passed for agreement following successful results during an earlier voluntary pilot where 80 per cent of tests taken prompted admissions from paedophiles and rapists.

The most commonly used technique in lie detection procedure is the control question test of CQT. In CQT, three sorts of questions are asked: neutral, such as 'Are you Fred Bloggs?'; key questions, 'Have you been unfaithful?; and control questions, 'Have you ever fantasised about another woman?' While these questions are asked the polygraph measures the individual's breathing, blood pressure and skin resistance. The control question should be designed to arouse emotion and yet not be central to the investigation. Innocent participants should theoretically react in the same way to the key and control questions. Guilty participants will, in theory, react most emphatically to the key questions.

One thing I find amazing is the number of men who willingly submit to the evermore popular lie detector tests. I am regularly asked to visit a couple's house to carry out this kind of test. I ask a series of questions which have been prepared earlier by the suspicious partner and while doing this I test the target's blood pressure and vocal cords as they answer. Most of those I test are men; I find that wives offer the test to their husband in the form of an ultimatum: 'Take the test or I'll leave you.' The vast majority of test results suggest that the husband is lying. I presume the husband thinks he can fool the test by remaining as calm as possible. I see him taking deep breaths because he thinks it will make a difference, but it doesn't. When a person tells a lie the forming of saliva is restricted to the mouth and blood flow is restricted to tonsils and vocal cords. It's impossible to disguise the change of frequency.

As a matter of fact, in antiquity the Chinese would give a suspected liar rice to chew; if he spat it out he was innocent, but if it glued to his mouth he was considered guilty. The logic behind this test was based on the knowledge that fear inhibits the secretion of saliva, so the modern lie detector test in many ways replicates this early form of physical truth-seeking.

As I listen to Mrs Noble, I realise things can't have been all that easy for Catherine over the past three years. Her father, Mrs Noble's husband, holds a senior position at a large pharmaceutical company, and often works in excess of eighty hours each week – hence his absence from our meeting this evening. The family have moved all over the world over the past ten years and Catherine has switched schools seven times in that time. Her mother gets the feeling this may be contributing to Catherine's mental state and worries that she may have turned to drugs in consolation, or perhaps to 'fit in' with the new crowd of kids at the most recent school, a private school with fees in excess of twenty thousand pounds a year.

I'm not convinced a lie detector test in this situation is the best way to go, but Mrs Noble knows her daughter better than I do, so I agree to return the following day with my equipment and as I cross the shingle driveway to my car I wonder how on earth she is going to manage to persuade her wayward teenage daughter to submit to the polygraph test.

By the time I get home the place is empty. It's past one in the morning and I'm now truly knackered; I can't even bring myself to check the score of the match (which the following day I find out England won 5–1!). I crash out on my bed fully clothed.

When I return to Hawthorns the following day the gates are already open and Mrs Noble appears at the open doorway looking very anxious.

'Thank you for coming, Mr Martinez. Catherine is in the sitting room; do come in and meet her.'

I follow Mrs Noble through into a large L-shaped room, leading onto a beautiful, wooden conservatory. The room is stunning, with plants that look like they've been pinched from one of the greenhouses at Kew, Oriental wood screens, and a Persian rug the size of a swimming pool. The surroundings are bright and cheerful and contrast starkly with the tense, claustrophobic mood permeating the room. Catherine is sitting on the edge of a wicker chair covered in bright flower-covered cushions and barely meets my gaze as her mother introduces us. She is a tiny girl, small and thin. I can't see her face; her almost-black hair hangs down across her eyes, her personal security blanket, and falls onto her shoulders like a dark veil. Her hands lay tightly clasped together in her lap as she perches on the edge of her seat.

I try to put her at her ease by explaining a little about the polygraph test and how it works. It has to be said it's a painless procedure – well, physically painless that is. The emotional stress and consequences that often follow a test can be a whole lot more painful.

'Right then, let's get this over with shall we?'

I work through a series of 'control' questions interspersed with a few 'relevant' questions.

'Are you pregnant?' 'Do you have a boyfriend?' 'Are you taking drugs?'

I feel very uncomfortable posing the questions. She shifts around in her chair and I can tell it's agony for her. I am pleased I asked Mrs Noble to leave the room prior to starting the test. Initially she wanted to stay but I want to ensure that the test is as valid as possible and therefore removing Catherine's mother goes some way to achieving this. Answering such personal questions in the presence of a complete stranger is difficult enough for anyone, let alone with your mother staring at you.

Catherine, I decide, is an open book. I hardly need the polygraph to tell me that she's lying: it's written all over her face. The results are conclusive, but I make my exit before sharing them with Mrs Noble. I'll phone her when I get back to the office. In my early days I used to announce the results of the test straight afterwards, but now I telephone the results through from a safe distance away, otherwise the couple start arguing in front of me. The last thing I want is to subject Catherine to a showdown with her mother in the presence of a complete stranger.

When I phone the results through, Mrs Noble answers on the first ring, obviously anxious to hear the news. I give her the good news first: her daughter is not pregnant, or at least isn't aware of being pregnant; She has never knowingly stolen from her father and isn't hooked on drugs.

Mrs Noble's relief is palpable, even across the airwaves.

'I'm afraid the rest isn't so palatable, Mrs Noble. It would appear from the test that your daughter has stolen from you, and she's skipping school very regularly.'

Although I get the feeling she is relieved to hear her daughter isn't an addict, Mrs Noble can't rest until she gets to the bottom of her daughter's secret life. She asks me to take any action I need to get to the bottom of it.

'I'll do what I can, Mrs Noble. Leave it with me. And try not to worry.'

'How long will it be before I get the report, Mr Martinez?'

This is one question I simply can't answer, but I assure her I'll be in regular contact and feel sure I'll have a result within two weeks. I fear Mrs Noble won't hold it together much longer than this and resolve to get to work first thing in the morning.

I slump into bed early and read through Catherine's diary, given to me by her mother. It reads a little like a list, and certainly without the emotion or details I'd expect from a girl her age. I suspect it's a bit of a smokescreen for the benefit of her mother. Why else would she leave it lying on top of her dressing table for Mrs Noble to find? I close the diary and drop it to the floor. I'm too tired to analyse it any further this evening, so I turn off my reading lamp, switch my phone to silent and roll over onto my stomach. As sleep slowly overtakes me, the events of the evening start racing through my mind and the image of Catherine keeps appearing before my eyes. After an hour of thrashing around, bashing my pillow and shifting into all sorts of positions I decide enough is enough; I fire up my laptop and get to work obtaining some background information for my new case.

Since Catherine is, at least in theory, at school five days out of seven, I decide the best way to keep tabs on her is by attaching both a listening device and a tracking device to areas of her clothing. I drive over to Kingswood first thing on Monday morning and post the devices through the letter box, warning Mrs Noble to expect them. I instruct her to place them somewhere Catherine will be close to all day, maybe in the lining of her rucksack or on the clothes she is likely to wear to sixth form college; in the hem of her skirt or waistband.

Around 10 a.m. I don my headphones and listen in to the audio receiver, apparently sewn hastily into the hem of Catherine's skirt at 8 a.m. today. The reception is fairly clear and free from crackles, so I assume Catherine is inside a building; perhaps she went to school after all.

I can make out faint music and a man's voice in the background, probably a fair distance from Catherine. Colour fills my face as the sound of grunting fills my ears and I feel embarrassed for the young girl; I must be listening to her going to the toilet. Out of decency and respect for my client I'm about to pull the headphones off my ears when I hear the same man's voice say clearly:

'Move then, you frigid bitch, help me enjoy it for fuck's sake.'

With horror I realise that sexual intercourse is in action. As the sound of flesh pounding into flesh floods my ears, my mind races – trying to form a picture of the events taking place. Why is Catherine in close proximity to a couple having sex? My experience of listening devices tells me the male voice is clearly a distance away from her; it's fairly faint and today's devices pick up sounds very effectively. Any sound close to the device can be heard distinctly. My imagination leaps from scenario to scenario and it occurs to me in a moment of dread that Catherine must have removed her skirt; she is the object of this man's attention and it doesn't sound as if he's being at all gentle.

Listening in on such a private moment disturbs me more than I would have imagined. The majority of us hide away to make love for the same reason we shut ourselves away in a small room to carry out our bodily functions: human beings crave privacy and respect. At the moment I'm abusing that and I'm not at all comfortable with it. It's the ultimate humiliation for her. I console myself with the conviction that this girl needs help. As my thoughts race to piece all the information together I conclude that this is definitely not passion at work, not for the female anyway, and it's not lovemaking either, I'm certain of that. By the time I reach my office I've heard enough to hazard a guess that Catherine's heart certainly wasn't in the events I've been party to.

I feel soiled by the experience and desperate to find out what's going on with this girl. I'm struggling to imagine why on earth a pretty young school pupil would subject herself to sex with a man who showed so little regard for her.

With some reluctance, I take out my mobile phone and open up the tracking application I have installed on it. My mobile works with the tracking device that has been sewn into Catherine's clothing, and within minutes I'm looking at a map which tells me exactly where she is. After what I've just heard, it's vital to find her quickly and make sure she's safe. I'm quite certain the encounter Catherine had wasn't with a schoolboy or a college student; the man sounded older – much older.

The tracker tells me Catherine is in the Rose Hill area in Carshalton: an average suburb nearby renowned for more than the average share of chavs. I head there on my motorbike, and after nearly being knocked down by a boy racer in an Escort I find myself outside a row of narrow, run-down terraced houses.

The tracker indicates Catherine is inside one of three houses, but I can't determine exactly which one.

I've barely parked up and taken my helmet off when the tracker shows movement. Catherine exits one of the houses and appears on the street, looking utterly miserable and marching so quickly down the road that my tracker can barely keep up with her. She's wearing an expensive looking tweed grey skirt, black jumper and tailored black jacket, and she looks like exactly what she is: a rich kid dropped in the wrong part of town.

God, she looks unhappy. And old. I'm not sure I've ever seen a sixteen-year-old look so grey and downtrodden. Aren't schooldays supposed to be the happiest days of your life?

I follow her on foot to the nearby railway station, keeping far behind her, and as soon as she's safely on the train I double back on myself and head to the house she just left. Up close, the residence has a cold, lonely feel to it. From the cracked concrete path to the corroded aluminium window frames and battered front door, it's clear this is a house that hasn't had a penny spent on it for quite a few years. It looks more like a squat than somewhere anyone would pay to live.

I note the house number, and head back to my office to run a full check on the person who resides in the property: name, occupation and criminal record. I want to know everything.

As I zoom around the narrow streets and back to the office, I think about Catherine. Why is she seeing a man who clearly has such little regard for her? It didn't sound to me like the pair knew each other at all, as they hardly spoke during the encounter.

Back at the office, I'm no closer to answers, but my check on the house is revealing some interesting information. Apparently, the property is owned by a Mrs P. Philips, a landlady who rents several other properties in the Rose Hill area. I find a newspaper article from five years ago that links one of her properties to a drugs raid, but after that, nothing. Discovering who lives in the property

Catherine was visiting is proving difficult. Whoever resides at 72 Moorland Drive isn't on the electoral roll. After a very roundabout search, I eventually manage to find a number for Mrs P. Philips on a lettings advert, and give her a ring – under the pretence I'm interested in one of her properties.

I place the call and she picks up immediately.

'Hello?' she squawks, not sounding at all happy to be disturbed.

'Hello, Mrs Philips,' I say. 'The house in *Lettings Today*. Is it still available?'

'Yes, yes,' she screeches, at a pitch I'm sure only dogs should be able to hear. 'It's still available, yes.' She says the word 'available' like it's an agonisingly long word she wishes she didn't have to bother with. 'You want to look at it?'

'Um… I'm not sure yet. I got your number from a friend of mine; one of your tenants. He lives at 72 Moorland Drive.'

'Bri-an?' she trills.

'That's him,' I say. 'Brian Smith.'

'Brian Smith? No, no,' she says irritably, and I imagine her waving her hand at the phone receiver as if to shoo me away. 'You mean Brian Knight.'

I ask a few more questions about the property she has for lease, and then make a polite excuse about needing more bedrooms, before hanging up. Brian Knight. OK, so it's only a name, but at least it's a start.

It's mid-afternoon, and my tracking and listening devices tell me Catherine has returned to school and is sitting through an A-level maths lesson. As she's safely out of the way, I decide to check her home computer. The housekeeper lets me into Hawthorns, and Mrs Noble shows me through to Catherine's large bedroom, which is tidy and pleasant and has a nice view over the family's large garden. I spot her laptop straight away and turn it on. Since the computer is actually the property of her mother I am legally allowed to instruct her how to access and copy the information; I have to be very careful to stay within the law when snooping through the personal devices of others.

With my advice, Mrs Noble gets to work scouring the hard drive of Catherine's computer. If there's one thing I've learnt in my role as PI it's that sinister activities always leave a trail and that trail is usually lurking on a SIM card or hard drive. I suggest she begins scouring 'My Documents' and after nearly five minutes she comes up trumps with an encrypted file she's unable to access. We try a few passwords that may appeal to a teenage girl, but give up after 'McFly', 'Girls Aloud' and 'Amy Winehouse'. My mind draws a blank; I'm way out of touch with the teen scene. I may have to hire a professional hacker to open this one.

We decide to open all the files we're able to and read every one to try and get inside Catherine's mind. As Mrs Noble leaves to prepare some fresh coffee I settle myself down for the long haul and begin browsing through hundreds of saved Word documents. Catherine has saved lots of poems, presumably written by her, and their content gives a clue as to her mental state. She's clearly a very unhappy girl. The poems are written unflinchingly, from the heart, and I'm moved by the depth of emotion they contain. One reads:

'I am on a journey into the unbelievable,
where pain and loneliness reside...'

What quickly emerges as I read is a picture of a girl who doesn't know where to turn. My hunger to find out more increases and as I work my way down the list another document catches my eye. Marked 'Clients', I'm hoping it's not encrypted and, bingo, it opens and brings up a list of names: 'Jack', 'Legolas', 'Drew', 'Paris'. The names are obscure and don't fit with the names of any pupils at the school or anyone Catherine has daily contact with. Maybe they're code names? I study the list again but there's no apparent connection between them, until I realise they're all characters played by Orlando Bloom in his screen films. That's it! Not so out of touch after all.

With rising excitement, I set aside my notebooks, type 'Orlando Bloom' into the password box, hit enter and – nothing. I try 'Orlando' without success and then 'Bloom'. Another failed login! Bugger. I puzzle over the list again and another possibility occurs: 'Pirates of the Caribbean'. Within seconds of hitting enter the password box disappears and a list of names typed into a Word document fills the screen. The list is separated into two columns: the left-hand column is headed 'Done', the other 'To Do'.

Each name has a phone number listed beside it. I could carry out extensive enquiries on the numbers and discover the full name of each person it belongs to, but that could take a while, particularly if it's a pay-as-you-go mobile phone, and I figure it's best to try the old-fashioned way first. Eagerly, I scan the columns looking for a name I might recognise. One name jumps out at me from the very top of the 'To Do' category and almost stops my breath: 'Brian'. Maybe it's Brian Knight? There are no surnames listed, but if it is him this list is a whole lot more sinister than it first appeared.

Trying not to be too hopeful, I lift the phone and dial Brian's number. The area code tells me I'm calling a line that could be in the Rose Hill neighbourhood – the suburb Catherine visited earlier this morning. After six rings, a gruff voice answers.

'Yeah?'

'Good afternoon, Brian,' I say, in my best telephone voice. 'I'm David, calling from your gas supplier, and I have some good news for you.'

'Yeah?' He's not the most imaginative of speakers.

'You've qualified for a 20 per cent gas discount this month. Can I just confirm the spelling of your surname?'

'K-N-I-G-H-T,' he says. 'Is that it? Can I go now?'

'Thank you for your time, Mr Knight.'

I hang up the phone. This case has suddenly got very interesting indeed.

As the end of the school day draws near, I leave Hawthorns and head to Catherine's school so I can observe what she does when she leaves. Before long, I'm sat on a bench around the corner from Reigate Manor and have placed the listening receiver back into my ear. I can hear a lively history teacher talking about the Second World War, a few pupils whispering and lots of pens scribbling on paper. It's a relief that Catherine is where she should be, but when the bell rings I brace myself. Will she go straight home?

I hear excitable teenage voices as the class is let loose for the evening, and strain to discern whether Catherine is talking to anyone or not. She's been very quiet throughout the afternoon, and I'm beginning to wonder if she has any friends at all. As school pupils troop past me, I spot Catherine among them with her head down and eyes fixed on the floor. Not only does she not have any friends, but there's no danger of her making any with that sort of body language.

Suddenly, Catherine vanishes from view, and I peer at the moving throng of children, trying to work out where she's gone. The listening device begins to crackle and I hear the sound of paper rustling. It sounds like notes being exchanged.

'Sixty.' It's a boy's voice, and he must be standing right next to Catherine, wherever she is. He sounds delighted.

Where is she? I stand and take a good look around. The boy continues to talk.

'You've got the list, yeah?' he says. 'How many more clients this week?'

'Three.' It's Catherine, and she sounds frightened and close to tears.

'Good girl. That's a hundred and eighty quid. Don't cry.'

But she is crying. She's sobbing, in fact, and now the crowd of school pupils has dissolved somewhat I can see her huddled by the fire exit of an office block, talking to a tall boy with red hair.

'Stop it!' The boy slaps her, and Catherine is instantly silent. 'You're seeing another one tomorrow, yeah?'

'Yes,' says Catherine, her voice barely a whisper.

'That's good.' The boy bends down and kisses her on the cheek. 'I'll take care of you, all right?'

Catherine nods, and manages a smile. Then the boy leaves. He bounds along the pavement towards the underpass, unaware he now has a PI on his tail.

Later that evening, I arrange a meeting with Mrs Noble. Something has to be done before tomorrow. My pursuit of the red-haired boy, whose name is James, turned out to be very fruitful indeed, but there are now things Mrs Noble needs to know about her daughter that can't wait. As I pull in through the gates at Hawthorns I close my eyes and take a deep breath. This isn't going to be easy.

'Catherine's upstairs,' Mrs Noble tells me, as I'm led into the sitting room. 'Please. Tell me everything.'

Without saying a word, I hand her a printout of the encrypted 'To Do' list I found on Catherine's computer earlier today. Mrs Noble examines the list carefully before giving me a blank look.

'These names mean nothing to me, Mr Martinez.'

'Catherine is in some trouble,' I tell her, wishing I'd thought harder about how to phrase what I'm about to tell her. 'There are some kids at her school who are into drugs. Hard drugs. Cocaine.'

'But the lie detector test said—'

'Catherine doesn't take drugs,' I interrupt. 'The lie detector test was right about that. But she's earning money for a group of pupils who do. They're demanding she pay them protection money, and then using the cash to feed their drug habit.'

'So that's why she's been stealing.' Mrs Noble sounds relieved, as if all the pieces of the puzzle now fit together. She hasn't heard the worst of it yet.

'This group... they need a *lot* of money,' I say carefully. 'Hundreds of pounds a week. Catherine has been... well, she's been seeing men. This group have set her up as a call girl, so she can get them the money they need. Men are paying her to sleep with them, and she's giving the money to this group of kids.'

Mrs Noble's mouth drops open. There's a long pause, and then tears start streaming down her face. She looks wretched – as wretched as Catherine.

I pull out some good shots of the red-haired boy buying drugs from a well-dressed twenty-something man in a graveyard near Catherine's school, and then some equally good ones of James and his friends snorting white powder from the cover of a maths text book in some local woodlands.

'My plan is to give these to the police,' I tell Mrs Noble. 'But it won't be an end to Catherine's problems. She's miserable, Mrs Noble. She has no friends, and once this gang are dealt with, she'll more than likely be picked on again.'

Mrs Noble nods, wiping dark mascara from under her eyes.

'I'll leave you to think things over,' I tell her, placing copies of the photos and other evidence I've gathered, including a written transcription of everything I've listened to, on her coffee table. I wince as I imagine Mrs Noble reading the part detailing noises of a sexual nature, but she wanted the truth and now she has it.

Three months later, I call Mrs Noble to see how she and Catherine are doing.

'Catherine is much happier,' Mrs Noble tells me. 'We've sent her to workshops that help her cope with bullies. And those pupils... the ones who took money from her... they've been expelled. I hear they're attending therapy.'

Neither of us mentions Catherine's method of earning money. The police have evidence of Catherine's encounter with Brian Knight, along with the list of names on the 'Done' list. Catherine was legally past the age of consent when the events took place and, although she felt she had no choice, she wasn't physically forced into complying with the bullies' requests, so whether the police have any power to act or not is anyone's guess. I don't ask Mrs Noble about it – I imagine the less she has to think about it the better.

'I'm glad she's happier,' I tell Mrs Noble. 'Very glad.'

The journey through adolescence is one of the hardest we ever make and the scars gathered along the road from child to adulthood can last a lifetime. If my early intervention in the lives of just a few teens helps their parents steer them along a safer path I'm a happy man. And as George Orwell said, 'No one can look back on their schooldays and say they were altogether happy.' But at least now Catherine can finish the last of her schooling without being afraid, and I'm keeping my fingers crossed that by the time she leaves school this year she'll have made at least one friend.

5

URBAN MINEFIELD

'It's so unlike him, Mr Martinez.'

I've had so many anxious parents say this to me I've lost count. Sitting across the desk from me is Derrick Williams, a middle-class gentleman in his early fifties. Derrick is fairly typical of the parents I've been employed by over the past three years: hard-working, respectable and worried that their young John or Annabel won't be following the straight and narrow path they've been led down for the early years.

'We've always been so close, I just can't understand it. James has everything going for him, why would he turn to drugs?'

Derrick explains that his son has grown increasingly secretive over the past few months, leaving the house at unusual times.

'It happened again last night. We were sitting watching TV when his mobile beeped. I asked who it was and he snapped, "No one." I said, "Don't be ridiculous, how can it be no one?" That was it; he stormed out of the room, took his coat, left the house and didn't get home until the early hours. When I checked on him this morning he'd fallen asleep fully clothed. I'm convinced he's on drugs. Why else would he behave like that out of the blue?'

'Maybe he's being bullied by someone, or perhaps he's being manipulated at school? Then there's girl trouble or gangs? It could be anything with a teenager...' I find most parents automatically assume their young 'John' or 'Jessica' has turned to drugs if they're having problems. I suggest other possibilities to try and help Derrick consider all the options before I take him on as a client. It's sometimes easier to identify problems looking in from the outside, and I've found some parents get so anxious they can't see the wood for the trees. I charge fifty pounds an hour to track an individual, be it an adulterous spouse or a wayward teenager, so my services don't come cheap. Having said that, Derrick seems like a pretty clued-up sort of bloke.

'No,' Derrick shakes his head, 'there's something wrong, I know it. Please help him, Mr Martinez.'

I had a hunch James hadn't joined a gang; none of the tell-tale signs were there, such as the sudden and unexplained appearance of new possessions, graffiti tags on schoolbooks, change in language and use of slang words, or a change in physical appearance – I think if James had arrived home from school wearing a bandana Derrick certainly would have mentioned it. James had remained committed to his usual after-school interests and activities and his school grades remained excellent. I know from experience the signs of negative influence from joining a gang, as the impact on a teenager is immense; but James isn't displaying any of them.

Less than forty-eight hours later, I call Derrick and tell him I've discovered the secret his son hides and my initial suggestion was correct, partly anyway – he is involved indirectly with a gang, only his son isn't a member. Derrick leaves work immediately and within half an hour of our phone call he sits across the desk, ashen-faced and anxious for the full story.

'Your son didn't go to football training last night, Derrick. He took the train to Longmead Estate in Epsom and there he bought Lidacane tablets from a member of the Riverview Crew, a local gang dealing in all sorts.'

'The selfish, ungrateful little bastard.' Derrick buries his face in his hands.

'It's not what you think, Derrick, he wasn't buying it for himself.'

'What?' He looks up sharply, his eyes still shining.

'He buys it for his mother.' I let the silence take over and give Derrick time to absorb the information. He stares at me in shock and gradually the truth dawns on him. The signs he missed, or perhaps chose to ignore, all begin to make sense.

When he discovers his voice again, Derrick reveals his wife is an ex-alcoholic who has battled all her life with depression. Her problems grew worse after the birth of their children but, with Derrick's help, she managed to dry out and he thought her addictions were a thing of the past.

'Doesn't he realise what he's doing to her?' I can see the pain in Derrick's eyes and I have a hunch the anger he feels at being the last to know may be directed towards James.

'He's trying to help his mother, Derrick – it's the only way he knows how.' I decide to play part of the tape to Derrick, to help him understand the impossible position his son has been in over the past few months.

'Your wife has grown more and more dependent on the drugs, Derrick, and her monthly prescription is no longer enough for her.'

James's adolescent tone fills the room as I hit the play button. First his voice is pleading with his mother, asking her to get help from her doctor – telling her he'll support her, go with her, sit down with his father and explain her difficulties. The sound of sobbing fills the air, then his mother's shaky voice tells him she only needs him to do it for her this one last time, and then she'll be strong enough to start withdrawal.

'You said that last time, Mum.' James sounds placatory and it's clear he'll do as she asks.

I think Derrick has heard enough.

'Poor James.' Derrick rubs his forehead, the full picture sinking in.

'It just didn't add up, Derrick. I knew from experience he wasn't the one taking something – the use of drugs screws people up, particularly kids. Your boy was something else. His latest school report was excellent; he remained committed to his athletics training, turning up diligently three times a week for practice. I knew he couldn't be using the stuff himself. The quickest way for me to find out the truth was to listen in on exactly what was going on.'

Derrick shakes my hand and thanks me for finding the truth. As he leaves the office I consider the fact that he leaves with a whole different set of problems than he first thought. That's the strange thing when seeking the truth and hiring my services – the client often unearths more than they bargained for. He now realises his relationship with his wife is at breaking point, but he has a model son who would do anything for his mother, rather than a drug addict who's joined a gang.

It seems when teenagers are involved, most people are ready to think the worst. Having watched some teens in action on the streets I can understand why, but at least my client still has enough love for his child to turn to me for help. In the American state of Nebraska, hospitals regularly take in dumped teenagers, dropped off by their parents who've reached their wits' end. A state law over there offers immunity from prosecution for parents if they hand the children safely into drop-off points at local hospitals. The law was originally passed to protect newborns who might otherwise be abandoned on the streets, but since Nebraska set no upper age limits, their hospitals are swarming with uncontrollable teenagers who are then passed on to foster homes.

It's not always parents who come to me with problem teenagers, however. It's barely a week since Derrick left my office, when I take a call from Mr Adamson, chairman of the Tabor Court Residents'

Association. Bill, as he asks me to call him, has lived in the area all his life and seen many changes since the early 1940s, and, he tells me, most of them aren't positive ones. Life at Tabor Court has had its ups and downs over the years and they've had their problems, but over the past year it has reached crisis point. It seems the youths have banded together in a gang and they are terrorising the neighbourhood and all its residents.

I agree to take on the case and my heart sinks as I take down the address. It's in one of London's less desirable spots, Tower Hamlets, the kind of deprived urban area that makes a fertile breeding ground for gangs. Mr Adamson has called an Extraordinary General Meeting for the Residents Association of Tabor Court this afternoon and I tell him I'll meet him at the community hall for 2 p.m.

As I step off the train I'm grateful I've dressed down for the meeting – anyone in a suit would be a target for pickpockets or muggers in this kind of area. I receive a few suspicious looks as I pass by a couple of groups of young people lurking around the platform, and as I make my way out of the station I notice barely a single section of concrete is clear of graffiti.

The community hall is one of the many 1970s buildings thrown up to offer council tenants 'modern luxury', but now looks decidedly sad, dated and in need of a paint job – or a demolition ball. I'm ushered into the hall by a well-built young man who stands taller than I am. It's all very 'cloak and dagger'. He glances nervously up and down the street before closing and locking the door behind me.

I'm directed towards the middle of the room where a group of I guess about twenty-five people sit around a large conference table. A man in shirtsleeves rises from his chair to welcome me and shake my hand.

'Richard Martinez, sir. Pleased to meet you.'

'Hello Richard, so pleased you could come. I'm Bill.'

After sitting with these people for just a few minutes I realise they are scared out of their wits, and all by a bunch of schoolboys and girls, average age of fourteen years.

'It just wouldn't have happened in my day, Richard,' says Bill. Bill is a retired police officer who spent thirty years patrolling the local streets on the beat. Now, he tells me, he is no longer able to leave his house after dark.

'Years ago we used to give kids like these a clip round the ear, take them home and their parents would do the same. Now it's the kids who attack the police and we're so namby-pamby with them, they get away with it. The worst of it is the parents would do the same: they're anti-police, anti-community, anti bloody everything. I never thought I'd see the day, I really didn't. There's just no respect left.' He shakes his head in frustration. I get the feeling he'd like the opportunity to take them on.

'The silly thing is, most of the kids around here are OK. They get a bit bored, but there's nothing nasty about them. There's a problem with a minority, but the impact they have is huge.'

An attractive young woman timidly raises her hand to talk and I nod to her encouragingly.

'I feel like a prisoner,' Tina tells me. She can be no more than twenty, twenty-two maybe, and yet she hasn't been out in the evening for over six months. 'I'm trying to save for a car. It's the only way I'll feel safe travelling around here.'

Tina also tells me that her young niece picked up a hypodermic needle while playing in the local park, and now her sister is terrified she may have become infected with HIV. The little girl has been tested negative but the fear never quite goes away. I realise the kind of pressure these people are living under; there is no quality of life and drugs seem to be a big problem here.

I nod, and scribble notes on my pad, trying to take in as much detail as possible. As the meeting draws to a close, I sense everyone is waiting for me to say something. Thanks to my regular radio appearances I am able to speak with confidence to a large audience and have been told my voice carries the weight of authority. I clear my throat and get to my feet.

'If I can get together some strong evidence of crimes being committed,' I say, lifting my voice a touch, 'I will pass it on to the police, and hopefully they can make some arrests. If the ringleaders are prosecuted, chances are the trouble will stop – or at least calm down.'

The group seem delighted with this rather lukewarm offer, and Mr Adamson leaps up and shakes my hand.

'I believe we'd like to hire you,' he says, and over his shoulder I see nods of agreement from the other residents. Everyone looks happy. They must be really desperate for something to be done. I say my goodbyes, wishing that these people didn't have to hire me out of their own money, but I'm pleased to be of service.

As I head back to the station, I pass a grubby-fronted estate agents, the greasy windows festooned with equally grim-looking properties, and I grab a copy of the local paper from the rickety stand leaning against the wall outside the shop. If I'm to find out exactly what's been going on in the estate I need to be where the action is, and my cover needs to be authentic.

At the station, I'm eyed up by loitering teens and it's not a comfortable feeling. I'm very glad once I hear the familiar rumble as the train nears the station. Boarding the train I feel a little humiliated at what a relief it is to be safely aboard. No wonder the residents of Tabor Court don't feel safe in their own homes. I've been in all sorts of situations most people have never even imagined and am a bloke who can take care of himself, and yet these 'kids' have the power to make me feel threatened. Paradoxically, I believe it's their age that is most disquieting; their behaviour can be so unpredictable without the necessary maturity.

During the journey back to Wallington I have enough time to phone and secure myself a room for £120 a week, including bills.

An advance from the residents of Tabor Court should be winging its way into my expenses account right about now, so there'll be more than enough to cover it. I'm not expecting anything too luxurious, and haven't gone for an expensive choice since the residents have clubbed together with their own hard-earned savings to try and make their lives more peaceful and stress-free. It won't help them if I fritter their savings on glamorous digs. Mr Adamson offered to put me up for as long as it takes to wrap up the case, but if anything goes wrong it will make him a vulnerable target and I don't want that. Besides, I'm expecting to be out all hours of the night.

Back at home, I pack enough clothes for at least a week away and stuff them into my scruffiest rucksack, my laptop jammed down the side. Other PI paraphernalia, including night-vision glasses, trusty zoom-lens camera and video equipment, goes into an equally grubby-looking holdall; I don't want to become a target for thieves on my return journey and no one would guess there's £10,000 worth of equipment in the scratched-up Adidas bag.

I tell my new landlady I'll be arriving after seven this evening, so I have a few hours before catching the train back to Tower Hamlets. I fire up my desktop and set to work brushing up my knowledge of the London street-gang scene. It makes frightening reading. In 2006, the Metropolitan Police found there were 169 youth gangs in London alone, many using weapons including firearms. It is estimated the gangs were responsible for 40 murders in the capital and 20 per cent of all youth crime during this year. On the poorest housing estates, ones just like Tabor Court in Tower Hamlets, up to 70 per cent of the residents are from ethnic minorities and levels of youth and adult unemployment are among the highest in the country. Segregation along the lines of race and economic factors led to 'ghettos' in the USA and it seems we may be following the same pattern over here.

Many gang members turn to an easy and lucrative source of income: sale of Class A drugs. Kids in these gangs form a part of the supply chain often working for unknown 'faces' at the top of the pyramid. The faces, sometimes known as 'elders', are usually adult members of crime families, operating in the background to protect their identity and maintaining contact with drug importers and other professional criminals. Their past is chequered with extreme violence and they are faceless forces to be reckoned with. Their reputation silences would-be whistleblowers.

The activities of the youngsters (usually aged between thirteen and eighteen) are expected to protect the market their gang creates and prevent other gangs taking their territory, give early warning of police presence, patrol the boundaries of their estate to protect from rival gangs, collect drug debts on behalf of the elders and undertake street crime and burglary for the elders.

Aside from serving those further up the chain, 'youngers' as they are sometimes known, engage in street crime for their own amusement. Girls often play an ancillary role, hiding weapons or drugs for the boys. Senior gang members are respected and it is thought that girlfriends of members are passed between each other and sometimes offered to the whole group. Rape is rarely reported, although it is feared to occur frequently. Typically, young people are enticed into gangs between the ages of twelve and fourteen, although some members can be as young as nine or ten. Many are attracted through simple boredom or join to protect themselves against threats from their peers. Unaffiliated young people in the borough often become subject to intimidation, harassment, theft, violent assault and sometimes rape.

After my meeting with the residents of Tabor Court, I'm aware some of the above is occurring daily in their neighbourhood. I can only surmise just how bad it's got on the estate. It's about time to make my way over there now and find out exactly how deep the problem goes. The train pulls into Wallington station just as I step onto the platform, and within fifty minutes I'm trudging along Pitcairn Way with my rucksack over one shoulder and holdall over the other, wearing my oldest pair of trainers and torn jeans. Not a good look, but neither is a beaten-up face after a mugging.

After taking a quick recce of the area, I spot a girl, around her mid-twenties I'd guess, hair pulled back into a tight ponytail, baggy tracksuit bottoms, off-white trainers and a tattoo that reads 'Frankie' across her flabby white midriff. I congratulate myself on my chameleon ability – I blend in perfectly with my surroundings.

As I head along the road to my new temporary home, number 29, I hope it will be in a location not too far from the action. The bars at the window give some indication that I may be in luck; I don't need to draw on my detective abilities to deduce that. As I make my way along the cracked pathway I notice the front door stands on two brick-built steps, the red paint chipped and peeling. The door itself is scarred, I guess from years of careless tenants. After ringing the doorbell I'm wishing I'd packed some wet wipes in my scruffy holdall; there's something extremely unpleasant caked around the rim and it's sticky enough to cling to my fingers. This is the sort of place where you wipe your feet as you leave, not as you walk in.

As I shake my hand vigorously to remove the gloop, I hear footsteps. There's a sound of several bolts sliding back then the door opens a few inches, the length of a chain lock. I spot one eye peering out to examine me.

'Hello, Mrs Gunn? We spoke earlier. It's Mike, Mike Brown.'

The door slams abruptly but I can make out a faint tinkle as the chain is released and when the door finally opens I'm confronted with London's answer to the she-devil. My new landlady, Val Gunn, stands before me, a living, breathing advertisement for why mutton shouldn't dress as lamb. Her dyed, jet-black hair hangs in scraggy sheets around her hollow cheeks, and a tight, glittery vest top reveals bony shoulders and a wrinkled cleavage. A pale blue skirt with a dearth of material reveals legs shot with varicose veins. She's smeared bright-pink lipstick over her thin lips, and she greets me with a gappy, yellow-toothed smile. I haven't even got the door open before she's grabbed my arm and pulled me inside, looking me up and down with her watery, blue eyes and giving me a leery wink, as if to say, 'Where have you been all my life?' I'm pulled into a semi-embrace with her as she leads me into the house, and I smell cheap whisky and even cheaper perfume. If I lit a match right now, I think she'd go up in smoke.

'*Do* come up,' she says, in what I fear she feels is an alluring, smoke-parched voice. 'I've got your bed ready.' She lowers her voice on the word 'bed', and looks me up and down again. Now I'm wondering whether the bars on the windows are to keep trouble out or keep her in. 'And if you ever get lonely in the night,' she adds, 'I'm just down the hallway.' I decide not to say anything, lest I encourage her more.

Val demands two weeks' rent upfront, something she didn't mention over the phone, but I hand over a wad of notes without argument or hesitation, if only to get her out of my room. As she leaves, I lock the bedroom door using the key she gave me and slide the bolt across too. I may be six foot three and built like a semi-detached, but the thought of Val in a drunken stupor leaning over me at 3 a.m. is not my idea of fun.

By the time I've unpacked my rucksack it's getting dark and since there's not much I can do confined to my room I set off on foot, armed only with a tiny digital camera, the size of a credit card. I can keep the camera tucked in the pocket of my jeans – wandering around this estate with a highly expensive zoom-lens camera is going to get me noticed and probably mugged into the bargain.

I'm not really sure where to head first: all seems pretty quiet as I leave the house and walk along Wingford Road. I guess if I stroll around for the evening I'm bound to come across at least some of the gang members. Sure enough, within minutes, like a pack of hyenas, five youths swagger around the corner and pass me on the other side of the road. They're too busy swearing and pushing each other intermittently into the road to pay much attention to me, but already I've snapped a couple of shots of them with my credit-card camera. Since they seem to be making a nuisance of themselves already – howling, using foul language and pushing each other into the path of moving vehicles – I decide to do a U-turn and follow them, from a distance of thirty yards or so.

They make their way into the square forming a large courtyard in the middle of four large blocks of flats, although this is more like a concrete jungle than a courtyard. The blocks are typical of the 1970s; forty years ago they were no doubt welcomed as a more appealing alternative to unsanitary nineteenth-century crumbling buildings preceding them but over the past twenty years have deteriorated to the point where they are simply a dumping ground for people who have nowhere else to go. A quarter of the flats are boarded or derelict and the rest look like the walls may crumble if splashed with a coat of paint – perhaps that's why the local council haven't attempted a revamp.

The group of youths, all boys, swagger across the square and loiter in one of the dimly lit 'tunnels' leading through to other blocks. It's staggering to think the designers of these buildings gave so little thought to the practicalities of housing. So many people together in minimal space – did not one of them consider they were building a breeding ground for crime, with so many alleys and tunnels for people up to no good to hide? It may have been built in the 1970s when London wasn't in the grip of youth knife and gun crime as it is now, but even so the capital had problems, albeit on a smaller scale.

Barely ten minutes since I've left my room and the memory card of my tiny camera is almost full as I snap the youths getting busy 'decorating' the tunnel with graffiti. No longer lethargic, they swing into action and work so quickly there's barely any blank wall left. As I watch them work I try to keep track of which youth does what – an important way of linking each 'tag', or graffiti logo, to a particular person. As they leave, I give it a couple of minutes to make sure the coast is clear – I want to record each tag and try to link it with each gang member.

I see this dirty graffiti-covered wall as my starting point – a way of identifying each member of the gang. Gangs use graffiti as a means of communication. What I need to do is use the street-level intelligence I gather as a means of tracking the youths. It is estimated that the annual cost of graffiti to the capital alone is in excess of £100 million. If I can do my bit to nab the culprits in this area, the residents will be pleased and it'll save the taxpayer at least a few pennies in funding the cost of major clean-up operations. If I can link just one offender with one graffiti tag, they can be held responsible for all the other damage they cause.

Pleased with the start I've made on my first evening, I decide to pop back to Val's via the kebab house I passed earlier, located only minutes from my room. I don't generally go for a kebab, but when in Rome…

As I round the corner into Pitcairn Way, the smell of spit-roast lamb fills my nostrils and, I have to admit, kicks my taste buds into action. I realise I haven't eaten since before I took the call from Bill this morning. That's what happens when I get stuck into a project, I lose all track of time and focus on the business in hand. But then I hear anguished but muffled screams coming from the wasteland area behind the row of run-down shops, and as I get nearer I realise there's a girl in trouble back there. It's far too early in the case to blow my cover charging to the rescue – I'm supposed to be an unemployed layabout who spends his days looking for a way to make easy money and his nights on planet gaga due to drug and alcohol binges.

Having decided within seconds of a ploy to both help the girl and maintain my cover, I bluster clumsily through a short alleyway and charge over to the girl who is pinned to the ground by a male, her leggings down to her ankles. I'm singing 'Valerie' as noisily as I possibly can, in a slur I imagine to be far more noticeable than Amy Winehouse's on a Saturday night.

The man is momentarily distracted, and to my relief the girl uses the opportunity to push him off and make a staggering run for it, pulling up clothing as she goes.

'Oi!' The man turns to me, and gives me a hefty shove.

'All right, mate?' I slur. 'Got any dope?'

This seems to confuse him momentarily, and he looks me up and down.

'Sorry, mate,' I say. 'I didn't piss your girl off, did I?'

'Never mind about her, man, she's a slag.' Pete (and I refer to him in this way only because he has a tattoo on his arm telling me that's what he likes to be known as) dismisses her with a wave of his hand.

'Why do you say that? Do you reckon I could have her?' I say in a half-hopeful, half-leering tone in an effort to entice him into giving more information.

'She'd have anyone, man, no offence, no offence to you I mean, but she's a smack head, she'd do anything for that shit, man – not many people can chase the dragon and walk away, it's too good man, far too good.'

'But she didn't look like she's gagging for it. I know bitches like that. Was she prick-teasing you – winding you up?' It sickens me to join in on this disgusting banter, but sometimes the only way to get information is to join low-lifes on their own level.

Pete chuckles and looks pleased with himself. 'Na, course she wasn't willing, she wanted the shit first didn't she, but I can't get hold of any just now.'

I realise I've just landed an admission of attempted rape, as the sound-recording device sewn into the collar of my scruffy T-shirt will have picked up every word. Whether it can be used as evidence is doubtful since I've obtained it through covert means, but at least it will give the police something to go on, coupled with the snaps I managed to take earlier with my night-vision camera as I zigzagged over to them across the wasteland.

'What's her name?'

'What is this shit, man, do you want to fucking marry her?'

'No, but I want to give her my babies.'

Pete finds this hilarious and we throw our heads back, laughing in unison. I instantly shoot up a couple of notches in his estimation – I can see it in his eyes.

I decide not to pursue the matter. I don't want to arouse suspicion and it's an effort to disguise my disapproval.

'If you're feeling the horn, man, you need to get yourself over to 17 Tabor Court right about now, there's a fucking rainbow party going on tonight – I'm sure you could join in if you have the readies and there'll be dust there too.'

'Think I'm a bit pissed,' I slur. 'I'm going to hit the sack.'

'Come over tomorrow afternoon. I might have some dope for you then, man.' He gives me his address.

As I leave the alley, I remind myself if my PI work ever dries up I must apply for an equity card and pursue a new career on the stage. I've just managed twenty minutes in Pete's company as sober as a judge, and he thinks I've downed ten pints.

As I'm creeping back to number 29, an incoming plane makes its steady descent towards Heathrow, passing over my head with a ground-shaking roar. Lovely neighbourhood – the kind of place you could get beaten to a pulp and no one would hear a thing. Even in the scant light from the streetlamps dotted along Wingford Road the sight of Val's place fills me with gloom. The house needs flooring and starting again; the walls are out of plumb and the roof looks ready to give up the ghost before too long. An overgrown elm with branches that now appear to have become part of the house isn't helping matters. I ease my key into the lock of the front door and tiptoe up the stairs; I want to make it to my room without another encounter with a lipstick-smeared Val. With the skill and concentration of an SAS soldier in action making a silent approach, I reach the top of the stairs and almost collide with Val, lying in wait for me. She stands with a cigarette in her mouth, her legs slightly apart, and one hand on her hip, wearing what can only be described as a skimpy black frilly negligee. Scant and sixty aren't my idea of the perfect match, unless you're Lulu that is, and from where I'm standing Val and Lulu don't have much in common. Although if she gets any closer I am going to *want to shout*! One thin strap dangles precariously on the edge of her shoulder, threatening to slip down at any moment...

'Well hello, my love,' Val breathes huskily, placing a hand on my shoulder then tracing a finger down my T-shirt, finally poking me 'seductively' in the tummy.

'Sorry, Val, I'm not feeling too well.' I dash past her, feigning sickness.

Once in the safety of my room I set to work researching 'rainbow' parties, since I've no clue what on earth they are. When Google pops up with 333,000 results and leave me in no doubt as to what was going on at number 17 I begin to worry this case involves something far more worrying than a spot of teenage vandalism. Marshalling my concern, I decide to channel it into solving the case so that I can move on to something far more palatable such as run of the mill infidelity or bribery and corruption.

The site at the top of the list describes a rainbow party as a group sex event, popular with adolescents, involving oral intercourse. Basically, girls wear a number of different shades of lipstick and take turns fellating boys in sequence, thereby leaving a 'rainbow' of various colours on numerous penises. According to Deborah Tolman, director of the Center for Research on Gender and Sexuality at San Francisco State University, 'This "phenomenon" has all the classic hallmarks of a moral panic. One day we have never heard of rainbow parties and then suddenly they are everywhere, feeding on adults' fears that morally bankrupt sexuality among teens is rampant...' According to the Center's report, teenage girls enjoy the competitive aspect of the event by using the lipstick to 'mark' the depth of oral penetration, treating the sex play as a contest of sorts. With the unhappy knowledge that all this is going on just a few houses away, I fall into an uneasy sleep.

It's early afternoon, and I'm sat on a stained carpet tile in Pete's flat watching him pirate DVDs. He's using two recorders, connected to an old TV with scart cables that look decidedly rodent-chewed. He's just offered me a pirate copy of *The Lion King*, and I'm doing my best not to laugh at the idea of this raddled old drug dealer flogging Disney classics.

'Have you got anything a bit stronger?'

Pete shrugs. Shrugs are a major part of this chap's vocabulary.

'You know, anything a bit tasty.'

'What do you mean, man?'

'I'm talking about stuff you can't get in the shops.'

'If you're talking kiddie stuff or any of that shit you can fuck off out of here now. I ain't into none of that shit, man.'

'No, course I didn't mean that, I'm not either.' I'm beginning to see there is some sort of moral code going on here, just one I'm not familiar with. Despite Pete's harsh surroundings, at least he draws a line somewhere.

I sit with him for the entire afternoon, turning down his offer of a smoke, claiming a hangover from the night before. What I want to do is get to the main man, the bloke supplying Pete and his cronies with the drugs that they then pass to teens in the gang. Why do I assume the supplier is a man? Because in my experience he almost certainly is. There's no denying the fact that it's men who commit the majority of most damaging crimes in society: murder, rape, drug rings. No, I'm sure of it: a man is behind the plethora of drugs flooding into the area and I need his name.

In some situations when I'm trying to extract information from a 'mark', I play what I call 'the quiet game'; the idea is that human nature usually dictates any silence should be filled with noise and most people feel obliged to fill silence with inane chatter. I listen and use silences like an automatic weapon. Most people can't bear silence; they feel overwhelmed. All I have to do is sit back and watch them crack under the pressure. Often this leads to them giving themselves away. In this instance, Pete beats me hands down at my own game and stays silent for so long it's me who feels under pressure to talk. He grunts replies periodically, but nothing that's going to lead me to wrap up the case and head for the hills. I have bigger fish to fry.

I return to sit with Pete every afternoon at his invitation. I get the impression he's very lonely, isolated not only from his family and friends, but in fact, the entire community, as a result of his life choices; his only 'friends' the drug dealers who would eliminate him at the drop of a hat if he causes them a problem.

He spends most of his time staring at the TV screen watching Jean Claude Van Damme movies and munching packet after packet of pork scratchings, but we spend time chatting now and again. He stops abruptly during any bloody shoot-'em-up scenes and gapes at the screen, concentration written all over his mawkish face. I make an effort to laugh when he laughs and swear regularly, trying to foster a sense of comradeship. My limited knowledge of psychology, gained through years of people watching, often helps me during a case and I know that one of the fastest ways to get someone to feel at ease and open up is for them to feel you are 'like' them. It builds trust between you. And I need Pete to trust me if I'm to gain anything more than yet another offer of pork scratchings from him.

It's now Tuesday afternoon – eight days into my stay here. Once again Pete settles down in his cream and brown easy chair; cream being its original colour – the brown, I'm guessing, is a putrid mish-mash of cannabis resin and nicotine stains. Hospitable as ever, Pete offers me a roll-up and a packet of pork scratchings. I'm beginning to think that my daily excuse of not touching the stuff (both the scratchings and the roll-ups) until evening is wearing a little thin, but I have a hunch Pete is enjoying my regular company too much to question my behaviour and, even though I say so myself, I am playing the part of ragged old druggie well enough to deserve a golden mask at the next BAFTAs. And we're in for a treat this afternoon, he tells me. I need to dig, dip and draw on every ounce of acting ability left in me to stop myself from screaming with laughter at his DVD offering this afternoon. At least Pete has the decency to look a little sheepish as he shoves the disc into the recorder; the dulcet tones of Roy Orbison fill the sitting room and Pete grudgingly admits he is a bit of a Julia Roberts fan. I furtively study his face as he watches the romance develop between Edward and Vivian – I swear I see the glint of tear in the corner of his eye on a few occasions.

A strange and unwelcome feeling momentarily creeps over me and I recognise it as a mixture of fondness and guilt. I actually think I'm beginning to 'like' Pete in a peculiar sort of way. He has a childlike quality about him that can be endearing. I can hardly believe I'm feeling empathy for a drug peddler but I suppose if you spend time with a rattlesnake eventually you'll come to like it. I feel a touch of guilt at 'enjoying' hospitality courtesy of a man I am hoping to help put behind bars but the feeling doesn't last long. At least he can watch as many DVDs as he likes in Belmarsh, though I doubt he'll get away with *Pretty Woman* in there.

Halfway through the film Pete presses the pause button and rushes off to the lavatory; I can hear him in there straining. It sounds like constipation, which isn't surprising; it's clear he is a drug user and some drug abuse symptoms include constipation. However, Pete's discomfort gives me a golden opportunity as he has left his mobile phone sitting on the table in front of me. I pick it up quickly and dial my number into the phone. My phone is already on silent so as soon as it vibrates and I know the call has connected, I ring off. I then look for his dialled calls directory so I can delete the call. I am hurrying and a bit fingers and thumbs but I needn't worry. I am being serenaded by Pete on the throne as his painful rendition of one or two of the rather dodgier tunes produced by some of the 1970s new wave bands resonates through the flat, interspersed with the groans accompanying his discomfort. By the time he comes out from the loo, sweating, the phone has been back on the table for a couple of minutes and I now have a drug dealer's mobile phone number to share with the police later. They can use it to see who he is in contact with on a regular basis and start building a picture of his associates and possibly his customers.

Around 5 p.m. Pete strides out of the room and the sudden movement after hours spent glued to his chair (apart from his painful sojourn to the loo) makes me anxious. Maybe I've asked one too many questions and pushed him too far, raising his suspicions. My guard raises as he re-enters the room holding something in his hand, but I relax when I realise it's only a dish. Pete is thin and wiry, not an ounce of fat on him, probably a result of little food and lots of stimulants. He looks a little like an anorexic Rowan Atkinson, standing there, though his IQ in comparison leaves a bit to be desired.

He lays the dish of bright blue china, delicately painted with tiny bluebirds, on the coffee table and I resist the urge to laugh out loud as I recall my grandmother serving Sunday tea on an almost identical tea set, only she was serving something Mr Kipling would have been much more likely to approve of, instead of three grams of Charley.

'Who says crime don't pay?' Pete almost chokes himself with laughter as he moves the dish directly in front of me, almost lovingly, the way a mother lays her newborn in the cot for the very first time.

'Help yourself, mate, it's new stuff just in – it's good, man. I'll bag some for yer before yer leave if you've got some dough.'

My mind races for an excuse. 'I don't do this shit, man, strictly dope.'

'I got some of that too, man, you can take it with you,' Pete offers quickly.

'Would love to, man, but I ain't got no readies on me at the moment,' I reply, hoping that will put him off. It doesn't. He goes into the other room again and quickly returns with a slab of what looks like a lump of off-colour liquorice. But I know it isn't. It's a nine bar of cannabis resin.

'This is good shit, man. You gotta try some when you is flush.' He leaves the room and returns minus the nine bar. My mind is racing. So far he has offered to supply me cocaine and cannabis. Two offences. If I am to keep from breaking the law myself here I am going to have to use all my experience and know how to avoid it happening.

I watch as Pete scoops some powder onto a small mirror and uses a razor blade to chop up the drug and prepare two lines for himself, delicately, as a cook prepares ingredients for an important dinner party, almost with a sense of pride. The look of anticipation on his face reminds me of a child waiting for daddy to hand over an ice cream during a day at the seaside. He takes a twenty-pound note from his pocket, rolls it up into a small tube and leans over the mirror pushing one end of the tube up a nostril. He inhales quickly and deeply then switches the tube to his other nostril before carrying out the same action.

'Ah! Wow!' he exclaims as he sits back and rubs his nose exaggeratedly. 'Man, that's good!'

I watch him, simultaneously revolted and fascinated. Pete starts to crack his knuckles while he paces to and fro in front of my face, and I feel sudden nausea rising and the sharp taste of bile hits the back of my throat. It occurs to me that the white powder lying innocently in the bottom of the dish in front of me is the reason some gifted teenagers destined for a life of success and prosperity turn their backs on their future and their families. Why the screwed-up homeless guys spend their days travelling the underground begging from strangers to make enough for their next hit.

I've known people who've done it and friends of friends who can't live without it. I've seen it but never understood it. Drugs have never held any interest for me; I've never gravitated towards anything more potent than the odd glass of red wine.

'People kill for this shit, man, and this is nothing compared to smack – have you done that?'

I shake my head as I am momentarily lost for words watching the high that he is experiencing right there before my eyes. I also decide that I don't want to give him the impression I am interested in any heroin; the last thing I need is an attentive Pete heating up some smack for me to try before I leave. I have more than enough chemicals pulsing through my veins after having breathed in the passive smoke from his 'herbal' cigarettes for the entire afternoon.

'Oh man, you should try it; smack sends you off most of the time mate; a week passes in a day. Makes you numb, man, it's like the weight of the world is off your shoulders.'

'Do you ever get any hassle from doing this, mate?'

'Na, no one gives me any shit, man, 'cause they realise I know how to hurt a motherfucker. So does my crew.' Pete's use of American slang makes me cringe; somebody please tell this bloke we're in Tower Hamlets, not Harlem. Why is he talking as if he's black when he's as white as sliced bread? The crazy thing is that the angry, aggressive young man in front of me is hugely insecure.

'The Big Man's coming around later,' Pete tells me. 'He might have some work for you, if you need it. A bloke like you – you look like you can handle yourself.'

I nod, taking advantage of Pete's urge to talk at a hundred miles an hour about anything and everything – particularly about how well he can handle himself and how he is like that (he crosses his fingers in front of my face) with the Big Man. For the first time that day he starts to talk. And talk, and talk. After half an hour, I've heard how Big Man brings the drugs onto the estate, how Pete and the other lads sell them on and how everyone hides it from the Old Bill. I'm pretty impressed by how clever it all is, and also impressed with myself for recording every word Pete says on the device sewn into my clothing.

Pete receives a call on his mobile. There is a short conversation and he hangs up and then says, 'That was the Big Man. He's on his way up.' I look at my watch and make a note of the time. Knowing that Pete received a call from the Big Man at that precise time will assist the police in pinpointing the main player. Once they've done this it's simply a case of analysing his phone traffic to round up all the minions below him, and perhaps those even higher up the chain.

There is a complicated rhythmic knock at the door that I assume is some kind of code between Pete and the Big Man. It is a reinforced metal door, de rigueur for all self-respecting drug dealers. It provides protection from the baddies who might be out to get him and the goodies that might be out to arrest him. Of course, both the goodies and the baddies have got to get through the minders and watchers that sometimes protect the dealers before ever coming up to the door. However, that depends how high up the chain the dealer is and as I didn't have to run the gauntlet of some thug with a bull terrier waiting at the entrance to the block I assume that Pete isn't high enough up the dealer food chain to warrant those levels of protection. Pete goes to the door, releases the bolts, unlocks the door and I hear the visitor before I see him.

'Peeeet. All right, geeze?' A man strolls into the living room and greets Pete like a long-lost brother. Despite his small stature, the man is a barrel of muscle and his shaved head is covered in scars. He has an eagle tattooed on his neck, and more tattoos covering both hands. Since he's wearing a long-sleeved shirt, I mercifully can't see most of his body but guess there's probably plenty more tattoos there.

A nimbus of fear wells in my chest as I realise how far into the lion's den I've ventured. Upsetting the Big Man would be tantamount to signing my own death warrant.

'All right, Big Man.' Pete grins from ear to ear, and gives the not-very-big man a slap on his hand.

'Paul and Levi are out tonight, so you sit tight and sort out anyone who stops by.'

The Big Man eyes me suspiciously.

'Who's he?'

'All right, mate.' I stick my hand out and the Big Man shakes it. 'Just a mate of Pete's.'

Pete nods. 'I thought he could help you out. He's a big bloke.'

Big Man nods.

'Maybe, maybe. Anyway. Everything all right here, yeah? Catch you both later.'

'I best be off too, mate,' I tell Pete. 'I gotta try get some more money together.'

Pete nods. The Big Man has already headed out the door, but I'm not far behind. I see him climb into a silver Mercedes, and I manage to get a few shots of his licence plate as he speeds away. Relieved to be away from the drug-addled moron and the close atmosphere of the flat, I gulp in a few big breaths of fresh air to clear my mind. After hours sitting with Pete I begin to worry I'll become as paranoid as he is. I head back to the flat, elated to be nearing the end of this case.

I crash onto my mattress at 2 a.m., desperate for some rest. Unfortunately I spend the night chasing sleep that only comes around 5 a.m., but I get up with my alarm set on my mobile at 6.30 a.m. I need to get going on wrapping this case up as quickly as I can. As I fire up my laptop to update my report I feel highly agitated and low, depressed even. But still, I get the photos and sound clips loaded onto the computer, and even manage to label and file them neatly. It's best I get it over with: today is going to be a long day.

I pull aside the grimy heavy curtains in my room and the grey sky outside my exhaust-stained window does nothing to lift my mood. I pack my things, and pray Val isn't in the house. The last thing I need in my fragile state is to have to fend off a flirtatious pensioner. Putting clothes into a zip-up bag is proving difficult enough. If I'm honest, what I'd really like to do is fall back onto the well-used mattress and just lie still for the rest of the day. I have to admit, this case has taken its toll. But I know I've got to get out and get on with things.

A quick check in the corridor tells me that, mercifully, Val is in the bathroom. I tiptoe quickly along the bare floorboards and down the stairs, almost running as I get to the front door. As I reach for the door handle, I hear movement above me and the bathroom door creaks open. Quick as a flash, I'm out the door and running down the street. I couldn't care less if Val knows I've done a runner without saying goodbye.

Five hours later, the police know everything. They've got names, sound recordings and photos that point them towards criminal activity, and more importantly the 'Big Man', who I'm certain is the 'elder' running things on the Tabor estate. They tell me 'Big

Man' will be under covert observation, and they're hoping for an arrest in the coming months. They also have details of the rainbow parties – the activity in itself is not illegal but at least they can check to ensure that everyone who takes part is consenting and adult.

I've managed to pop home and have a shave before my update meeting with Mr Adamson – it's the last thing I feel like doing but one of my golden rules to remaining professional is to look my best. In my job it's important to instil confidence in my clients and if I appear scruffy I won't be seen as being in control. Anyone who appears weak and desperate is easily dismissed; self-confidence is a priceless asset to take into a business meeting: 'the look of the eagles'. I meet with Mr Adamson at my office – I think it's best to avoid going back to Tabor Court for a while now, not that I'll miss it. I'm having a cup of tea with Mr Adamson, telling him the whole story – minus the details of the rainbow party, I spare both of us that ordeal – and he seems happy. He tells me my hiring fee was money well spent.

'It could take a while for the police to make an arrest,' I say, 'and even longer for everything to filter down. But I think things are on the up for this area.' And I truly think they are. It's a good feeling, and I've got to say I'd choose the feeling of a job well done over a drug high any day of the week.

6

STALKING STALKERS

In my line of business there are a disproportionate number of cranks who are suddenly possessed with an urgent need to call my office – a never-ending stream of them, in fact. I believe that during the past nine years I've spoken at least once to every crank, eccentric and crackpot in the south-east of England. Thankfully, I've become adept at recognising them in an instant. A few of them I'm now even on first name terms with.

I'm sitting in the home of one such crank right now. It's a bitterly cold winter's day, and I've taken the train all the way to Kensington, London, to pay a house call on the elderly Mrs Banfield, who tells me she has a matter of vital importance to discuss, but it must be face to face. This immediately set off my 'crank' alarm, as a number of, shall we say, more 'eccentric' clients refuse to have conversations over the telephone because they fear the line is tapped. I've even been contacted by lunatics who fear KGB operatives at work, but I have never been able to confirm their worst fears (not yet anyway), much to their constant dismay.

Mrs Banfield owns a huge house in Kensington, alongside the wealthiest residents of the capital, and I'm sipping tea in her sumptuous lounge, which is furnished with large oil paintings and a carpet so thick you could lose shoes in it, as I listen to her story.

Wealth, it seems, is not necessarily an indicator of sanity, and Mrs Banfield is obsessed with conspiracy theories, and utterly convinced every member of her immediate family is trying to poison her.

I listen politely as she pours out venomous tales of her despised relatives. Allegedly they visit her three or four times a week and always prepare her dinner and a cup of tea. She apparently always eats the meal, despite the fact that there's no doubt in her mind it's laced with dangerous chemicals.

'If I don't eat what they've cooked for me, they'll know I'm on to them,' she says. 'My daughter gets quite cross if I don't eat what she's prepared.'

Her plan is for me to hide in the walk-in larder in her large kitchen before her daughter's next visit, and record proof of her incontrovertible convictions. While we chat, she pours me endless cups of tea from a delicate pot painted with roses, and offers slices of rather stale-looking cake. I'm becoming desperate for a lull in the conversation so I can make my excuses and leave, so I couldn't be more delighted when my mobile phone starts to ring.

'Do excuse me, Mrs Banfield,' I say. 'I have to take this call so I'd better be on my way. I assure you I'll look into your complaint.' After all, there is a small chance that her suspicions are correct, although if that's the case she's doing rather well on whatever her relatives are giving her – she's a sprightly old thing.

As I find my way to the grand front door and let myself out into the cold, I take the call.

'Hello, Richard Martinez speaking. How can I help?'

It's a young lady called Sarah, and fortunately she doesn't fear infiltration by the KGB and is happy to fill me in on her problem over the telephone. It turns out she's been living under the shadow of a stalker for the past six months.

According to *Merriam-Webster's Dictionary of Law*: 'Stalking is the act or crime of wilfully and repeatedly following or harassing another person in circumstances that would cause a reasonable person to fear injury or death, especially because of expressed or implied threats; broadly: a crime of engaging in a course of conduct directed at a person that serves no legitimate purpose and seriously alarms, annoys or intimidates that person.'

When clients with stalkers get in touch, I know their case requires the utmost sensitivity and understanding. The recent stalking case involving the actress Uma Thurman highlights the distress these cases cause and a great deal of investigative skill is required to solve these kinds of crimes. Since people sometimes feel very uncomfortable involving the police in matters involving stalkers, PIs are used frequently to gather evidence that supports legal action against the perpetrators.

Of course, as a PI there is always a possibility that a stalker could hire me to do their work for them, and obtain recordings of an ex-lover for obsessive, unhealthy purposes, so I am very careful when I take on a new client to make sure they are not using my services for ill-intent. I always ask what the purpose of their snooping is, especially when men are involved, as according to studies around 90 per cent of stalkers are male, yet only approximately 20 per cent are victims. Most female victims know their stalker, and in fact nearly 60 per cent are stalked by their current or previous partner.

I have been approached by people I deem to be stalkers before, and asked to follow ex-lovers around, record the details of new love affairs or find out new phone numbers or addresses for an old flame. I would never knowingly take on a case of this sort, but sometimes stalkers conceal their intentions, telling me the person they'd like followed is a current girlfriend who may be cheating, or a long-lost relative. Since private investigations cost quite a bit of money, it's usually not too difficult to distinguish between a genuinely heartbroken husband who'll pay high sums to find out for certain whether his wife is cheating, and an obsessive ex who'll more often than not immediately lose interest when I tell him my charges.

Despite the statistics suggesting males are the main offenders, I try to keep an open mind and not become too blinkered. Women stalk too. I was approached a few years ago by a very attractive blonde in her mid-twenties called Jenny, who had just finished training to be a lawyer, owned a beautiful flat in the West End of London and outwardly appeared to have everything a woman her age could want. She asked me to find out all I possibly could about a middle-aged gentleman who lived in Chelsea, but was a little reluctant to go into detail, so I jumped to the conclusion that this man may be her long-lost father and she wanted to find out more about him.

Ironically, far from assuming that she was bothering this man with obsessive calls and letters, I thought she needed my services so she could work up the nerve to make contact with him. I have had a few cases like this, where I have managed to trace birth relatives for clients, only to find they are too scared to make contact. Their reluctance is sometimes alleviated once I find out a little more about their birth parents and this can often give them the confidence to make the initial approach. In one or two cases I have approached the family myself, sort of an ice-breaker to get things moving. But Jenny was adamant she just wanted information at this stage.

I got to work and prepared a file for Jenny. The gentleman in question, Christopher, was fifty years of age, married with two grown-up sons and worked from his home in Chelsea as a psychotherapist. With my experience today, as soon as I realised what he did for a living, alarm bells would set off and I would probably have figured out that Jenny was not Christopher's long-lost daughter at all, but an obsessed client of his – one that he had gently, but firmly, declined to have a relationship with. Back then I didn't know that females are much more likely to stalk current or former therapists than men. They often pursue their target in the search for intimacy rather than in pursuit of sex. Men are much more likely to begin stalking in an effort to restore an intimate relationship that has ended.

Once I handed the information to Jenny, she pored over it with the intensity of a mother examining her child's school report. She seemed very upset by the fact that Christopher had two sons, and even more distressed when she discovered he was married. She even whispered '*that bastard*' when she read about his wife, and I realised this was much closer to the behaviour of a jilted girlfriend than a long-lost daughter. Since my research into Christopher showed him very much as a family man and happily married, I began to wonder about Jenny. She was an odd sort of girl, despite her good looks and apparently successful position in life. She lived alone, although she had several spare rooms in her flat, and there were no pictures of friends or boyfriends around the place. Our phone calls were always much longer than they needed to be, and I got the feeling I was keeping Jenny company during our chats. When I asked her what her relationship was to Christopher, she burst into tears.

'He was my therapist,' she told me, 'and I thought he loved me. But he's left me, just like everyone else does.' It turns out Jenny was dealing with a fear of abandonment, and had become obsessed with her therapist whom she felt was the only person who understood her. I put her in touch with a local female-only counselling centre, and made her promise to get help – which she agreed to do.

Meeting clients like Jenny helps give me a unique insight into the thoughts and feelings of the stalker, but of course more commonly I'm given an insight into the distress and anguish felt by the victim, since I'm regularly contacted to help gather evidence of a stalker's criminal behaviour.

Why do people become stalkers and cause misery and fear in the lives of their victims? Ironically, in my experience the root cause in most stalking cases is love, or perceived love. Although males are more likely to stalk strangers than females, it is unusual for anyone to be stalked by someone they have absolutely no knowledge of or connection with. Substance abuse and criminal history are said to be common markers for potential stalkers, but by far the most prevalent predictor is prior sexual intimacy.

Some people are almost desperate to fall in love, and lots of people fall in love headfirst and at top speed. They don't question their feelings. All too often they lose control of them and they trust their partner without hesitation, so when a heady relationship ends this is often when the trouble begins.

Everyone feels sad at the end of a relationship. It's a normal, natural response to losing something that was treasured. Most people are able to deal with the range of emotions they feel, from anger and depression, to sadness and fear for the future. But a few can't deal with such powerful emotions easily. They resent the rejection they feel and become desperate to get back into the affections of their loved one. If they're unable to convince the one who spurned them to take them back and restore their injured self-esteem, the overwhelming resentment they feel can turn into obsession.

Stalkers become consumed by hatred and can think of nothing else. It inflames and destroys them. The person they have been spurned by becomes the focus of their thoughts. All their energies revolve around restoring the relationship, or exacting revenge, in an effort to alleviate the boiling emotions inside them. The creation of fear in the person who 'caused' their grief provides them with a sense of power that was taken from them when they were discarded. They revel in their newfound control and feed from it. It's a dangerous state of mind.

I chat to Sarah for about half an hour, accept her as a client and agree to meet immediately. She lives with her parents in North

London, so after a short train ride I find myself on a pretty suburban street of semi-detached 1930s houses, and approaching a family home with colourful pansies hanging in baskets around the front door.

As soon as Sarah opens the door, I can see the stress she's under. Aside from the fact she pulls the door open slowly and timidly, like a frail, frightened old lady, she has tired creases around her eyes and frown lines etched into her forehead. She's only a young woman, and I feel a great deal of sympathy for her. It looks like she hasn't slept well in months.

She manages a worried smile and invites me in, showing me into a cosy lounge containing shelves of books and a well-worn red suite. I take a seat on the sofa and wait while Sarah brings me a cup of tea, which as a matter of fact I could live without after the hot drink marathon at Mrs Banfield's, but I accept for politeness' sake.

She takes a seat opposite me, and says, 'I shouldn't be living here, at my age. With my parents, I mean. Four months ago I had my own place. It's like my life is moving backwards, not forwards.'

She begins to tell me her story, or rather her nightmare, which began six months ago.

The New Year brought with it big changes for Sarah. Having recently moved jobs, she moved into a flat of her own near Clapham South. One of the main attractions of this part of London, besides its close proximity to her new place of work, was the wide open spaces and green areas that surrounded her. Also, living near the city centre suited Sarah's vivacious, fun-loving nature and her parents were pleased to see her settled and making the most of her life. Coming from a close-knit family, she remained in regular contact with her parents and brothers, despite moving south of the river while they all remained north.

After a hard day in the office, Sarah loved nothing better than chilling in front of the TV with a glass of wine, the phone by her side, waiting for a call from her mother. Hardly a day went by when they didn't chat.

It was just a few weeks into the New Year when she met him. Sarah was sitting in the meeting room of the publishing house where she worked as a secretary, when she noticed a man staring. The feeling that she was being watched made her look up from the notes she was diligently taking, and she caught his gaze from the other end of the boardroom. Smiling fleetingly, she returned to her notes, but couldn't shake the feeling that his eyes remained on her.

After the meeting, the man strode straight over to her and introduced himself.

'Hi, I'm Andrew. I'm a marketing manager here,' he told her. 'You've been with us a couple of weeks, haven't you?'

Sarah hadn't noticed him before today, and was surprised he knew exactly when she had started with the company. After a brief coffee together, Sarah got ready to return to the office, but Andrew wasn't going to let the opportunity pass him by and asked her then and there to join him on a date. The pair had made a connection, he was sure of it – that certain something so difficult to define and so rarely discovered.

Although Andrew was over six feet tall with dark hair and attractive, manly features, he didn't instantly appeal to Sarah so she politely declined his offer. Later that afternoon he sent her an email repeating his request to take her out. Despite wishing he would leave her alone, she responded to the email and agreed to meet with him that evening. In these kinds of situations her good nature always overtook her first instincts. It wasn't part of her character to tell someone to bog off.

The date passed smoothly – enjoyably, even. And yet even at this early stage in their acquaintance Sarah had an uneasy feeling. Something wasn't quite right. Maybe it was the fact that he seemed to like her an awful lot. But then again, could it be that she didn't value herself enough to allow someone to adore her as he seemed to? Before the end of the evening he was already organising their next date. Her eagerness to please (an innate quality so prevalent in young women, and one that age and bitter experience sometimes manages to quell) overtook her again and reluctantly she agreed to meet him a second time.

During their first date, she had mentioned a family party organised for the upcoming weekend and, rather brazenly she thought, he invited himself along. Tired of being teased by her brothers for turning up to every event as a singleton, she agreed to take Andrew with her, if only to wipe the smug smiles from her brothers' faces.

Sarah's mother, Patti, took an instant dislike to Andrew. Female intuition told her something wasn't right, even though he was perfectly friendly and solicitous. Her mother couldn't quite put her finger on what it was about the man, but she felt uneasy. Never one to hold back on expressing her feelings, she told her daughter she was unimpressed by him, but immediately regretted her harsh words. Sarah was a strong-minded young woman with her own life to live. She should be free to make her own decisions and so Patti decided to remain quiet on the subject from then on. And yet one brief meeting with him had been enough to unnerve her.

Her mother's 'interference' irritated Sarah and she resolved to do exactly the opposite of what Patti wanted. For goodness sake, she was twenty-two years old: an independent woman with a good job and her own flat. When Andrew asked her out later that week she immediately agreed. He took her for a meal and then on to a local wine bar. Conversation was easy and they found many areas of common interest. They shared a love of books and travel, and talked into the early hours. Early misgivings faded with each glass of wine and she invited him back to her flat that night. As they kissed each other fully on the lips he thrust his tongue deep inside her mouth. Tugging at her blouse he slipped his fingers inside her lacy bra and with forefinger and thumb he tweaked her nipples.

She was later to find out from one of Andrew's many subsequent letters that, from Andrew's point of view, his initial conviction had been correct and the chemistry between them was tangible. The sex they shared was better than anything he'd ever known before. He felt confident that this was how it should be – he'd finally found what he was looking for.

Sarah's experience at the end of the night was rather different. She was never much suited to alcohol, and she knew after a few glasses of wine she often completely lost her head. And yet she hadn't drunk that much last night. Maybe the wine they'd been served was stronger than usual.

Locked together in a drunken and clumsy embrace, she knew she would regret it in the morning.

When they awoke, she raced out of bed and made Andrew a cup of tea. It was her signal that the date was over. Kicking herself for letting her guard down so easily, she knew she wanted him to leave. As far as she was concerned it was not a relationship she wanted to pursue, and having him in her bed had confirmed that. Busying herself with tidying the flat, she began to feel a little irritated as he sauntered around the place in only his boxer shorts. It wasn't right somehow. Despite their physical intimacy of the previous night, they barely knew each other. It had been a pretty clinical experience as far as she was concerned, and she just wanted to spend the morning alone.

After a couple of hours feeling like she'd just purchased a new puppy, her patience reached a limit and she asked him to leave. He refused. He did so jokingly, as though in an effort to keep the atmosphere light-hearted, but he refused all the same. Sarah was gobsmacked, and her initial suspicions about him were confirmed. Making a mental note, first to trust her instincts and second to take more notice of her mother, she politely but reluctantly tolerated the next few hours of being shadowed by him.

He finally left about 4 p.m., after she fabricated a tale about her brother coming for a visit. Recounting the events of the day on the telephone later that evening to one of her closest friends, Liz, she was urged to put an end to the 'relationship' immediately. Sarah considered Liz something of an expert where men were concerned and valued her advice enormously.

'You need to let him down gently,' Liz told her, 'and the sooner you do it the better.'

Taking the coward's way out, Sarah sent him a text to say she wouldn't be meeting him again. Despite the relationship being in its infancy, she felt huge guilt for rejecting him and so she made a comment in the text about hoping they could remain friends and she wished him all the best. About an hour later she received a text back and the chilling reply he sent turned her cold: 'I wish you dead.'

Terrified, Sarah swallowed her pride and confided in her mother. She was reassured by Patti that it was simply a knee-jerk reaction and no doubt the last contact she would have with the man, although secretly her mother feared the worst. And she was right.

The following day, Sarah was bombarded with text messages, thirty at least, some begging her for another chance, quickly followed by vile messages making all sorts of threats. Deleting them in disgust was the only action she felt able to take. Ashamed of the ease with which she had allowed him into her bed, she felt partly to blame for misleading him. All she wanted was to put the whole unfortunate episode behind her.

Sadly it was not to be. Her first mistake had been to reply to some of his messages. In an attempt to calm him she apologised profusely for any hurt she had caused and begged him to leave her alone. The following day the telephone calls began. As soon as Sarah answered, Andrew launched into a tirade of verbal abuse. Sarah ended the calls and, although shaken as a result of his aggression, was relieved that she had ended things before they went too far – or so she thought.

It was later that same day she received the first letter, which was equally as abusive as the telephone call had been. Shocked at its vitriolic contents, she calmed herself with the idea that once he had put his feelings to paper he would calm down and move on. But as a matter of fact, Andrew was feeling spurred on by achieving a response to his calls and his activities moved up to the next level. It was just the beginning of a long campaign of terror against Sarah, the effects of which impacted upon the entire family. He began following Sarah wherever she went, around the office and home at the end of the day. Liz advised her to report him to senior managers at the publishing house, but Sarah feared gaining a bad reputation and so remained quiet. After two weeks, she managed to secure herself a job at another publishing house and regretfully left her post, hoping it would help him to sever the ties and move on.

Unfortunately, by the spring of that year, just three months after their first meeting, Andrew had become a seasoned stalker. He followed Sarah everywhere. He quickly discovered her new place of work and she would spot him standing in the street below looking towards her window. He did the same at her home. Unable to feel safe alone any longer, she reluctantly put her flat on the market and moved back with her parents. For the first week after the move all was quiet, and it appeared he had finally lost interest. However, as far as he was concerned it was simply a little interruption in his activities.

Lulled into a false sense of security, Sarah planned an evening out with the girls – something she hadn't done since she first met Andrew months before. Things didn't seem quite right almost as soon as she left the house, though, and as she reached to open the door of her car, she recoiled as her fingers sank into dog excrement that had been jammed underneath the handle. Convincing herself it was the work of local youths, she cleaned herself up and made her way to the pub. Glancing over her shoulder as she stood at the bar, she spotted Andrew lurking in the corner of the room. Despite his efforts to keep his face turned away, she knew it was him immediately.

Whisked away without delay by her friends, they went on to their favourite haunt, a Chinese restaurant in Clapham. About an hour into the meal her heart sank when she caught sight of Andrew staring through the restaurant window. Her friends suggested they accompany her home. Fury built up inside Andrew as he watched a male sit in the passenger seat of Sarah's car. His jealousy and anger reached a peak. How dare she discard him like an old piece of rubbish, then take up with some other man? His depression grew deeper and he was determined to have his revenge.

Sarah said her goodbyes to her friends outside her parents' house, and they made their way to the local railway station. As she fumbled in her bag for her keys, she spotted something moving in the hedge surrounding the front garden. Tiptoeing across the lawn in her kitten heels, she gasped in shock as Andrew emerged from the bushes.

'How could you do it to me?' he whined like a child, then hissed, 'You dirty, disgusting slag, how could you want anyone else after me?'

Sarah screamed, 'Stay away from me! I'll call the police.'

Hearing her screams, her friends sprinted back up the road in time to see Andrew disappear around the corner and out of sight. Seconds later the sound of a car engine whirred into life, masking Sarah's crying. Never in her whole life had she encountered such venom from anyone and her body racked with the sobs of months of pent-up tension.

The following morning, after much urging from her mother, Sarah gave a ten-page statement to the police. Despite the two-hour interview, no attempt was made to interview her friends and no contact was made with Andrew. Although clearly a crime of harassment had been committed, it was difficult for them to take the matter further due to lack of resources and the sometimes wrongly held belief of some officers that the victim often brings these things upon themselves. Despite the best efforts of the police service in improving how they deal with allegations of rape and cases under the recent harassment legislation, there are still dinosaurs within the service whose attitudes let other more enlightened officers down.

The harassment reached a point where Sarah was reluctant to leave the house. Her stalker made a habit of following her, sometimes to work where he would linger outside for hours, or sometimes she'd see him waiting outside a shop she was visiting, but when she came out he'd have vanished. Her mother was worried sick every time Sarah left the house. Almost every morning there would be excrement posted through the letter box, and Sarah was convinced it wasn't the animal kind.

The police advised her to change her mobile phone number, as she had been receiving up to twenty phone calls each day and streams of offensive text messages. At first she had assumed that if she kept the same number, Andrew would eventually tire of receiving no response from her, but she made the mistake that so many victims of stalkers make: she ignored many of the phone calls, but every once in a while she would answer his call, simply to beg him to leave her alone. This signalled to him that his persistence was paying off and gave him even more incentive to try harder with his contact.

Once he was unable to contact her by phone, he bombarded the family home with letters, some offensive, some begging and pleading with Sarah to give him another chance. They had only shared three dates and one night together, but in his head there was an entire relationship going on.

A few days after his appearance at the restaurant, Sarah spotted Andrew once again crouching behind the hedge in the front garden.

Immediately telephoning the police, she screamed for them to come and help her. Having placed a special 'marker' on her address, they made the incident a priority and arrived within minutes of the call. After a thorough search of the area they found nothing. They left after giving her the usual advice: to make a note of all contact from Andrew and call 999 if she was in fear for her safety.

As Sarah finishes her story, she is visibly shaking and there are tears in her eyes. It's clearly been a long and painful ordeal for her, and it's also clear she still feels partly responsible for Andrew's behaviour.

There's a knock at the lounge door, and Sarah's mother pokes her head around the door frame.

'Is it all right if I join you?' she asks, and Sarah nods. Patti thanks me for coming and puts an arm around Sarah's shoulder.

'We just don't know what to do any more,' she tells me. 'I'm almost afraid to let her out of my sight.' She looks as stressed and tired as Sarah, if not more so. Patti tells me that she was the one who persuaded Sarah to get in touch with me, as she was becoming increasingly terrified that the whole situation would end badly.

I can see it's a great relief for both the women that I'm here, and Patti tells me she feels a great burden of responsibility being lifted from her shoulders. They're keen for me to make plans and deal with Andrew as soon as possible – straight away, if I can.

I'm pleased that both Sarah and Patti feel they're finally taking a positive step forwards, and I get started on Sarah's case as soon as I return to the office. Work is busy at the moment, and I should really only be taking on one case at a time, but this is one of those stories that 'touch' me and I desperately want to help as soon as possible – not least because I fear that Patti may be correct, and that Andrew may soon turn violent.

My first task is to find out as much as I can about the elusive stalker, who always seems to disappear before police arrival, so I camp out near Sarah's family home the next day and wait. It doesn't take long for him to show, and I recognise him immediately from their description. He's a well-groomed man with a long, straight nose and prominent jaw, and he looks every bit the business professional in his well-cut suit. That's if business professionals lurk on street corners, and follow their ex-girlfriends to work.

I follow him for the entire day, and find out where he lives, where he goes for his lunchtime pint and even where he buys his packet of fags.

After a few days, I manage to gather enough evidence to present to the courts for Sarah to obtain a restraining order, which means Andrew can't contact her or go anywhere near her home or place of work. This is one of the first steps in dealing with a case of stalking, and can sometimes be very effective so it's certainly worth a try. However, around 40 per cent of restraining orders brought against stalkers are immediately violated, and a large number of victims report escalating problems following the granting of orders, so I tell Sarah she shouldn't expect too much. We apply for the restraining order, and wait.

A few weeks later, I'm enjoying a cheese sandwich lunch at my local pub when Sarah calls. I'm not surprised to hear that although the restraining order has now been granted, it has had no effect on Andrew's behaviour whatsoever, and if anything he has stepped up his campaign of hounding her relentlessly.

I'm beginning to feel Andrew may be close to causing actual physical harm to Sarah, and resolve to follow him immediately – partly to get the evidence Sarah needs for a criminal prosecution, and partly to protect Sarah and make sure she doesn't come to any harm. What a case like this needs is a hands-on approach and often the police lack the resources to deal with the situation robustly, mainly because other crimes, those which, on the surface, appear to be far more serious, take priority. Worryingly, 54 per cent of female murder victims and 46 per cent of victims of attempted murder report prior stalking by the perpetrator to the police, and across all stalking cases one in five includes the use of a weapon for the purpose of threatening or harming the victim.

Andrew's stalking has become increasingly threatening and I fear that soon he'll try and hurt Sarah physically in some way, unless I work quickly. A priority for me is to prepare an intelligence file on the target, with the ultimate goal of collecting enough evidence to get a conviction.

I pack up enough kit, clothes and food for three or four days on the road and camp outside Andrew's home late on Friday evening – not the kind of long weekend I relish, but I'm hoping to get all I need within seventy-two hours.

I decide to spend the weekend away in my Volvo V40, which is no five-star hotel but at least there's plenty of leg room. And besides, Andrew lives in a well-heeled but family friendly area of the city – the kind of address where a Volvo blends in perfectly well. It's important not to stand out like a sore thumb if you're trying to gather evidence undetected.

I park with the front of the vehicle facing away from Andrew's home, and watch his front door using my rear-view mirror. This is tiring – much more so than straight observation of a target – but it's this sort of hard work that avoids my cover being blown, and good surveillance requires stamina, patience and subtlety if it's to be successful. It's not all chasing cars and setting honeytraps.

Just as I begin to lose all feeling in my backside, I spot movement. Andrew strides purposefully down his path, a mobile phone in his hand, using both hands to busily text as he walks. I don't need ten guesses to know who's on the receiving end of that message: Sarah tells me that since the restraining order, Andrew has somehow discovered her new mobile phone number, and she's receiving between ten and twenty obscene texts a day.

He heads straight for his Sierra, and continues to text as he starts the engine and pulls out onto the road. I'm all set to go, but make sure I capture his flouting of the laws against using a mobile while driving, just for good measure. If the weekend offers very little else, at least I have that – it's not enough to put him safely behind bars, but it's not bad for starters.

With a touch of déjà vu, I think how odd it is that someone like Andrew has become a stalker. I remember the surprise I felt all those years ago when I discovered Jenny, the beautiful, blonde twenty-something with a good job and lovely flat, was stalking her psychotherapist. Just like Andrew, Jenny appeared to have everything going for her, yet she became utterly obsessed with a man she hardly knew. You would have thought she had no reason to enter into a one-sided fantasy, and that she would be perfectly capable of winning a real-life relationship, but appearances of success can be deceptive.

Andrew is the same. On the face of it, he has it all: nice house in a decent (what estate agents would describe as 'sought after') area, great job, more than reasonable promotion prospects, sizeable assets of various kinds – and he's kind of good-looking into the bargain, even a bloke can recognise that. Why on earth is he wasting his life chasing after a girl who clearly doesn't want him? But if this job has taught me anything, it's not to judge by appearances.

As Andrew cruises along numerous residential streets I keep well back, at least two or three cars behind. It's vital I stay in the background and don't raise his suspicions at all. I'm relieved once he pulls onto the dual carriageway: mainly because I'm now sure he is making his way over to Sarah's place, so the hours staking him out haven't been wasted, but also because I'm able to pull alongside him rather than stay in the pursuit position. Shadowing a mark from behind can raise their awareness of your presence, as anyone up to no good usually checks their rear-view mirror continuously to make sure they're not being followed. If they don't see anything suspicious in their mirror they tend to relax, unaware that the more accomplished watcher will be driving parallel to their vehicle – or 'paralleling' them.

I'm so confident that Andrew is making his way over to Sarah's parents' house that I flick my indicator before he does, pull in a few cars behind him and then follow as he takes the next exit to leave the carriageway. Sure enough, he pulls into Fir Tree Road and parks up about fifty yards from Sarah's house. I carry on driving, overshoot Sarah's driveway and then pull in 100 yards further along the road. I set up the video camera and head on foot to get a little closer. I'm grateful for the leafy surroundings, giving me ample cover and allowing me near enough to get what I hope to be clear footage. I guess he's come over to deliver one of his threatening letters, or perhaps a foul-smelling parcel.

Busily concentrating on the focus and settings of the camera, I don't register that he's carrying a bat until I see him swing it forcefully at the living room window. The sudden shock of seeing this means I almost take my finger off the record button, but this is priceless footage and I hold on for dear life, resisting the urge to charge the twenty or so metres between us and pin the bastard to the ground.

He makes three or four violent swings with the baseball bat, then dashes away around the corner to his car. I'm confident that the footage is clear enough to identify him, but to make doubly sure I run to the end of the street and crouch behind the hedge in time to record him running to his car and slamming the door. I zoom in on the registration plate, then dash back to the house. I want to make sure Sarah and her family haven't been injured from the flying glass.

I continue to follow Andrew for a couple of days – in essence, stalking the stalker – and find out lots about him. It turns out he has a bit of a drug habit, so I video his dealings with his supplier and also film hours of him lurking outside Sarah's family home. Really, he makes it all too easy for me, and within a week I hand over a comprehensive file of evidence to the police. The next day Andrew is arrested, and although Sarah and her mother are ecstatic, we still don't know if he'll be put behind bars. Once again, there's nothing we can do but wait.

It's a sunny April afternoon, and I've just been given a wonderful piece of news. I thank the caller, a London police sergeant, for the information, and dial Sarah's number.

'Sarah. How have you been?'

'Great.'

She sounds it. After Andrew's arrest, the harassment simply stopped. Just like that. The constant texts and calls, the daily shadowing of her routine, all came to an end with one arrest, and slowly but surely she's building up her confidence again and resuming a much more normal life. And now I have some even better news for her.

'Andrew has just received a two-year sentence for harassment, threats to kill and possession of Class A drugs,' I tell her. The court have also made an order that prevents him having any further contact with Sarah even after his release. If he breaches it he risks returning to prison.

There's a pause, while Sarah digests this information. A long pause.

'Thank you,' she eventually manages to say, and her voice is glowing. 'Thank you so much.'

'You're welcome,' I tell her. 'But it was you who had the courage to get in touch. You should be thanking yourself, too.'

I hang up the phone, happy. I gain a great sense of satisfaction from getting a good result in a case, and love helping people and making a positive difference, however small.

The laws concerning stalking have been improved in recent years and it is now a crime to harass another person. It is, however, a crime that is very difficult to prove, and victims often feel they are making a fuss, particularly as in most cases the stalker has had a personal relationship with them at some point.

It's very important that victims take action, before things become too serious, which is why I'm always pleased when someone has the courage to get in touch with me and take a positive step before their stalker goes to extreme lengths to get noticed. Experience has taught me that taking the right action can put an end to stalking very quickly, and it's an enormous relief for victims and their families when the cloud of worry and fear is finally lifted for good.

7

SLEEPING WITH
AN ENEMY

When it comes to true love, I'm a cynic. I've seen a thousand movies about couples falling madly in love and living happily ever after, but my work as a PI means I also see the darker side of love and relationships. Infidelity, more infidelity and worse: domestic violence. Don't get me wrong – I believe in true love and happy marriages, but when you've seen what I've seen you'd be hard pressed not to take the idea of a 'true love' with a pinch of salt. I've had women arrive at my office with their arms or legs in plaster, trembling as they relay stories of beatings and psychological abuse at the hands of their partners. I even had one client who'd lost her three young children; they were taken into care by social services after being caught in the cross-fire of domestic violence once too often. She'd eventually managed to free herself from the domestic abuse and piece her life together but, sadly, there was nothing I could do to help this lady. Her intention was to track down her children so they could be reunited but it was simply too late; they'd been adopted on and were happy in their new life.

And it's not only women who are the victims: one client of mine was a gay man, whose partner would stub out cigarettes on his face and lock him in their flat for days on end. It can be very tough to deal with these cases, especially when I have to hear details of the humiliating, and often highly brutal, violence both men and women suffer at the hands of their partners. And more often than not, my clients will continue to suffer violence during the course of an investigation, which is something even the toughest PI finds hard to deal with.

It had been a while since I'd handled a domestic violence case, but then I received a hurried, whispered phone call from a woman called Sandra whose husband had become increasingly violent during their four-year marriage. When Sandra's call came through, I was on my hands and knees trying to fix the single oil heater I use to heat my office all winter. The heater and I have never been the best of friends since I took a hammer to it last winter when it kept turning itself off, and although the hammer seemed to do the trick in the short term, it's been temperamental ever since. On particularly cold days it likes to stop working completely.

But as soon as I answered the call and heard the trembling, frightened voice, the broken heater became the least of my concerns and I grasped the receiver as though it were a fifty-pound note in a storm. Sandra's voice was shaky and barely audible as she made a hasty request to meet with me. Although I had wall-to-wall appointments until the end of the month, she sounded so desperate, so fearful, that I knew I had to see her. She gave me a few details about her situation – telling me about her husband's split personality and the regular violent beatings she suffers – and we agreed to meet that day in a coffee shop not far from my office, in a discreet backstreet. The café is run by a lovely old Irish couple, Jack and Joan, who serve delicious coffee and bake the best fresh soda bread you've ever tasted. You wouldn't know where to find it unless a regular told you where it was, which is why it's a good place to meet clients.

I arrive a little early, driven by curiosity and a need to discover just what had happened to make Sandra finally seek help. Her voice sounded so desperate on the phone – pleading, even. I fear maybe her beatings have taken a life-threatening turn.

I spot her as soon as I enter the café. She's sat in the corner with her head bent down, chewing her nails and clearly trying to make herself look as invisible as possible. Her long arms are wrapped tightly around her waist in a childlike, protective gesture. My heart goes out to her at first glance. I decide then that it won't matter even if she doesn't have the funds to pay me. Whatever her story I know I have to help her.

She looks startled as I approach; I'm not due for another ten minutes or so and she's so absorbed in her own world of goodness knows what demons that she failed to register my arrival. As I get nearer, I notice how painfully thin she is, with large staring eyes and skin that stretches tight across her cheekbones. Her mouth twitches constantly as she chews away at the inside of her mouth.

'Sandra?'

She gives a tiny nod, and glances around the small interior of the shop before her eyes settle on the cushioned stool opposite her, as if to invite me to sit down. I take the stool, arranging my legs as agreeably as possible under the tiny seat and giving her a reassuring smile.

'It's much colder than usual for December,' I say, in a bid to get her talking about mundane things so she might relax a little bit. We talk about the weather, Christmas coming up and the usual first-meeting small talk, but every few seconds Sandra glances nervously over my shoulder and out to the street beyond. Her hands flutter constantly to her face, as if subconsciously wiping away the invisible tears she's afraid to shed.

'I used to love Christmas,' she says, and I get a good look at her eyes for the first time, as she gazes over my shoulder at the stubby little Christmas tree Joan has stuck in the corner. With her piercing blue eyes I guess she could be beautiful in different circumstances, but dwarfed by a far-too-big grey jumper, teamed with a bobbled cardigan that's wrapped loosely around her waist, she looks like a ten-year-old child with a vitamin deficiency. Ironically, she's wearing silver earrings that sparkle as she twitches her head, striking an uncomfortable contrast with the pallor of her face. She looks stricken with anxiety.

'I've never liked Christmas myself,' I tell her, in an effort to put her at ease and gently encourage her to reveal more about her problem. 'Good food, plenty of drink and piles of presents. I just can't stand it.'

Her mouth twitches as if to smile, and I can tell she's trying very, very hard to say something, but her mouth just won't shape the words.

'I'm terrible at buying presents though,' I continue. 'The shops see me coming. They know there are useless men like me around who just don't have a clue, and I end up with armfuls of those seasonal shaving sets or baskets of bath products.'

There's a pause.

'So, tell me about what's happening with you. You didn't ask me here to bore you with my small talk.'

Sandra catches her breath, and I think she's considering getting up and leaving. It's happened before: an abused wife suddenly decides she doesn't have the courage to seek help after all, and she backs out of a meeting never to be seen again. But instead, Sandra leans forward and begins to tell me her story.

'When I first met him, he was wonderful,' she says, 'a real gentleman.' How many times have I heard that before? As she talks, I recognise her struggle to retain control and keep her emotions in check. She speaks quietly, but with fevered urgency and the eagerness of a child.

'We met four years ago,' Sandra tells me. 'It was love at first sight. He was absolutely gorgeous. But it wasn't just that. He was warm and friendly; someone who would really look out for me.' She looks at the milky coffee in front of her, which she hasn't touched, and seems to be willing herself to carry on talking. I can see it's a struggle. 'I had a... difficult childhood. My real parents weren't the good sort, so I was put into care when I was three. After that, it was foster home after foster home, but I never felt like any of my foster parents really cared. Mark was the first person who ever looked after me.' She stares at the Christmas tree again. 'I suppose I'm very willing to give my heart away. All I've ever wanted is to be loved by someone.'

As her story unfolds, I feel more and more pity for the tiny young woman before me. It's a story I have heard all too often. The details vary, but basically it follows almost every other domestic violence case I have ever dealt with. Mark appeared to be the answer to her dreams. Strong and capable, he had a good job and was well liked by his large group of friends. A bit of a charmer, he was the sort of man who could walk into any pub and by the end of the evening be surrounded by admiring fellow drinkers. He'd be the first to buy a round and the first to jump to the defence of anyone in need. His pub mates described him as having a 'heart of gold' and in the early days Sandra would nod her head and agree wholeheartedly.

They married just eight months after they met and spent the first two weeks together in blissful contentment. Only then did the cracks start to appear. Subtly at first, almost intangible; the odd negative comment, one or two criticisms – easy to ignore really. When she became upset he convinced her she was being over-sensitive; it was one of her faults and a product of her life in foster care.

She knew he was right of course. He was older than her and better educated. She had left school at sixteen. Flitting from job to job, she had never managed to settle anywhere. When they first met she worked as a receptionist in a local company, but she wasn't very happy there. The work was tedious and Mark convinced her that she would be happier at home, taking care of the house. Providing her with everything she needed, he convinced her she had no need to work. They had enough money to pay essential bills and, anyway, she wanted to please him.

After a few months he began to object to her meeting up with the couple of friends she'd stayed in contact with from her childhood. He told her that she should break free from the past. He disliked her friends and felt that these people served as a reminder to her of being an unwanted child. He discouraged her from leaving the house during the evenings as he felt she should be spending her time with him. When she invited her friends back he gave them the cold shoulder, making it clear they were not welcome in *his* house.

Gradually she lost contact with them; it simply wasn't worth the battle. He was the most important thing in her life. Mark took care of her and her loyalty should lie with him. As the months passed his control over her increased until she was afraid to even think for herself. She checked everything with him and lost all confidence in her own ability to get through each day without him.

With her spirit broken she was barely able to object when the violence began. Again, it crept in slowly; a little shove now and again or a prod in the back when she angered him. She angered him often. After their first year of marriage the violence had escalated to a dangerous level, but she spent the next two years in a kind of daze, not recognising the situation for what it was. Fawning, she clung to him all the more, desperate to keep what had promised to be a relationship that would last forever. In the early days her manner changed whenever he was around; by now she behaved like a nervous kitten even in his absence.

A great hulk of a man, he had immense powerful shoulders and large hands. He always blamed her when he lost his temper, and until recently she accepted his condemnation without reservation. She loved him still and feared his loss of control. What frightened her most of all was the striking contrast in his behaviour when other people were around. No longer was he rough and brutal; he became loving and attentive. His whole manner changed, he even carried himself differently. The sudden change in his demeanour in the company of others was sinister because it was so unexpected.

Always willing to conform, she played along with the act – never considering that there was another way of doing things. The build up of abuse was so gradual that to her it simply felt like a normal way of life. Now her daily routine consisted of doing anything and everything she could to make sure Mark didn't lose his temper – but of course whatever she did was never enough. But a few days ago, things changed and for the first time she realised she had to do something.

'Why now?' I ask her. 'What's made you suddenly decide to seek help?'

She gives an unconvincing shrug. There's a reason, all right, but Sandra isn't going to tell me what it is – at least not yet.

Of course, just because she's broken the silence doesn't mean Sandra has suddenly become fearless overnight. She's experienced far too many years of abuse to stand up to Mark, or leave him just like that. But she has had the courage to seek help, and in me she's found the right person.

People often wonder why people like Sandra don't call the police straight away, and the answer is simple: they don't think the police will believe them. Sandra is scared that she won't be taken seriously and that her actions will simply anger her husband and fuel his violence: perhaps fatally so. As it happens, the police have become much better in recent years in dealing with incidents of domestic violence. Gone are the days when the police would refuse to attend a 'lovers' tiff' until the wife ended up in hospital, but it's not always easy to convince a battered spouse that this is the case.

Sandra has been convinced for years that there's no escape, such is the degree of hold Mark has over her. Desperate not to inflame his temper and too proud to admit to strangers that she has 'failed' to make her husband happy, just as she failed to make her parents love her enough to keep her, she keeps the misery locked away inside herself.

I try to convince her that the police should be her first port of call, but she looks terrified by the prospect, shaking her head with such aggression that the whole top of her body begins to shake.

'You don't understand,' she says, pulling her cardigan tighter around the shapeless grey jumper, which I'm sure is concealing an almost skeletal frame. 'He's like a different person around everyone else. He puts on an act. It's like he's two people. There's no way they'll believe me, unless I've got evidence and there's someone else with me who'll back up my story.'

I've seen this before: the Jekyll and Hyde syndrome. It's no surprise to me that so many Hollywood actors are accused of domestic violence, as Oscar-winning performances and abusive partners seem to go hand in hand. I went to court with a client of mine whose husband had been regularly beating her for years, and if I hadn't seen the bruises all over her body with my own eyes and recorded her husband smashing up their house in a jealous rage, I sincerely would have believed his innocence in court. He painted such a pretty picture of a devoted husband who had unfortunately married a vengeful, deranged wife that I began to think black was white.

'I feel like a bird held in a net,' Sandra tells me, 'totally helpless and stuck. Like there's no escape.' She falls silent, spent and exhausted from giving way to four years of pent-up grief. I'm sure she's going to cry, but she doesn't. Biting down on her lower lip she wraps her arms around her waist again.

I pity her a great deal, yet I also feel angry with her for losing so much control over her life. How did she let things get so out of hand? However, I quickly put my feelings to one side, and remain the practical, professional PI. I need a plan to secure Sandra's freedom and ultimately her safety from this man, and to instil in her some confidence, not only in my ability to help her, but also in her own long-forgotten capability to manage on her own.

'I'll help any way I can,' I tell her. 'But remember, if we don't go to the police right away the violence will continue while I'm collecting evidence.'

Sandra's jaw sets hard, and her bright blue eyes look to the ceiling for a moment.

'I don't think he'd beat me badly enough for something terrible to happen.' She says the last few words as though she's trying to convince herself there's nothing to worry about but I can see she's a woman who's hanging on to her self-composure by a thread.

'I don't like you taking that risk,' I tell her. 'But I can't make you do something you don't want to do. And I know how frightening this all is for you,' I lean forward, 'and how brave you've been in coming to me.'

She nods, stiffly, and I know she's holding back the tears.

'I do want to go to the police, eventually,' she says, her voice high and tight. 'But I need to make sure there's no doubt in their minds about what he's doing. Could you... could you put cameras in the house? So people can see what he's really like, behind closed doors. Not just the beatings but... the way he is, the rages. The storming around the house and the way he speaks to me, like I'm nothing.' She puts her head in her hands and gives way to sobs. 'I just feel like I'm going crazy sometimes,' she whispers through her fingers. 'Everyone thinks he's this big kind man with a heart of gold, who thinks the world of his lady wife. If only they could see how he treats me as soon as the doors are closed.'

I take hold of her hands gently, and move them away from her face.

'It's OK,' I tell her. 'I promise it's OK. You've done the hard part.' I explain how I'll go about getting the evidence she needs, and that we'll go to the police together.

She nods, and for the first time her eyes look bright and alive.

'Yes,' she says. 'I just want it all to be over; just all over and done with.' She lurches forward suddenly, and covers her mouth with her hand. Her face looks pale – green, even. 'Sorry,' she says, her voice muffled. 'Just the smell of coffee in here... I feel sick suddenly. I think I should get going.' I realise this has been a much more distressing meeting for her than it has been for me.

As we say our goodbyes she makes a tremulous effort at a smile, but it strikes a false, incongruous note coming from such a poor, tattered creature. Again I'm roused by a deep pity on her behalf and do my best to reassure her that she will be OK.

'Try not to worry; we'll sort it I promise.' I tell her.

She gives me one last glance of despair over her shoulder before scurrying away with her head bent low against the December wind.

The next day, Sandra calls me first thing.

'It's me,' she says, and although her voice still sounds frail and scared, there is a strength to it I hadn't heard yesterday. She tells me she slept properly last night for the first time since the downward spiral of her marriage.

'It was such a relief to finally share the truth,' she says. 'I feel good, now I know you can help me.' I love the feeling of instilling confidence in my clients.

'It's time to set the balance straight,' I tell her. 'I can't stand bullies. And do you know what? The funny thing about them is they love to dish out the dirt, but they're crap at taking it.'

This week, I'm absolutely determined to get enough evidence together to render Mark utterly defenceless in court.

After Sandra's call, I take previous case files involving domestic violence from my over-stuffed filing cabinet. Reviewing old cases helps me remember what works and what doesn't, and in a case as sensitive as Sandra's I want to make sure I've considered all the possible outcomes. At the end of each case I do a form of results analysis; I note the good and bad parts of each case and attach it to the cover to make reviews of my work more structured and organised. I also maintain a document on my computer that collates everything together.

The faded green cardboard files scrawled with clients' names look innocent enough, but inside many of them contain photos of trashed houses, bruised ribs and broken fingers. I've come across many 'Marks' over the past nine years, ruthless, dictatorial bullies who, interestingly, dissolve into paralysed humiliation once another man confronts them. As I sift through the files, the name 'Doug Stranger' catches my eye. Doug. He was a terrific guy, and a loyal, caring husband. It's not only men who abuse their partners. Doug's wife, Anna, had become very violent towards him by the time he swallowed his pride and called me. Although he was keen to stress that he wasn't afraid of his wife, he had lost almost all his self-confidence due to her violent outbursts and psychological abuse. Doug had begun to dread coming home, and was desperate to show Anna just how destructive her behaviour had become.

His wife was a successful estate agent who outwardly appeared to be a very together, controlled person who kept a tight rein on her emotions. She was a perfectionist in everything she did, and was the sort of woman who never had a hair out of place. When she and Doug first married, he loved the way she was so dedicated to getting everything right, and saw it as a lovely little quirk that whenever she bought anything for the house it had to match exactly the colour and style of the room it was going in. At Christmas time, if she received household gifts that didn't match, they went straight in the charity shop bag and it became a joke between the two of them that Anna was 'fussier than the queen'. But things changed when the estate agents where she worked started to have financial difficulty. The staff were increasingly pressured to sell houses and Anna would often stay out until nine or ten at night, cleaning and tidying the homes to make them more attractive to potential buyers. Of course, her perfectionism meant she had to get it just right – even if it meant spending hours scrubbing stains or mending broken fittings. She'd come home crying tears of frustration because there were marks on a cooker that she couldn't remove. And her Friday habit of a glass of wine after work to finish the week off became a daily habit of the full bottle.

One night, after two of Anna's sales had fallen through in the same day, she came home in a rage. Apparently Doug wasn't working hard enough. She did all the work, and Doug was useless and pathetic.

Doug stayed calm and carried on with his crossword, but that only angered her more.

She snatched Doug's newspaper and began hitting him around the head with it until there was nothing left in her hand but a clump of torn sheets. Then she burst into tears and apologised over and over again, telling Doug she wasn't coping at work and without him she didn't know how she'd manage. Of course, Doug forgave her, just like Sandra forgave Mark when the violence first started. It's so much easier to believe the best of someone you love, and believe a punch or a shove is a one-off, something your loved one only did in a passionate rage, and will never do again.

After that first incident, Doug told me Anna's temper exploded more and more regularly – always at home where they were both shut away from the rest of the world. She'd scratch Doug's face, or pull clumps of his hair out. If he wasn't home, she'd tear the house apart while she waited, and then throw crockery or shoes at him when he eventually came through the front door.

I flick through the photos of Doug's injuries, and the collection of medical reports we had written for him by a private health professional. And then I pick up the little memory chip that holds video footage of Anna's rages – the footage that finally convinced her she needed help. I'm hoping to create similar footage of Mark, although rather than using it to coax him into therapy, I intend to use it as evidence to bring criminal charges against him.

It's lunchtime, and I'm letting myself into Sandra's house with the help of the spare key she's left under the doormat. Understandably, Sandra's too petrified to let me into the house herself as she's scared the neighbours might tell her husband she's entertaining a strange man, so instead I'm visiting when she's out delivering Mark his lunch. She makes him a home-cooked meal and brings it to his work every day, which means she has a perfect alibi while I sneak into the house. If any of the neighbours notice a strange man on the doorstep at 12.30 p.m., no one can accuse Sandra of inviting him in.

The house is immaculate, as I knew it would be. I don't think there's an abused wife in the land who doesn't try to pacify her husband by making sure the house is spotless. It's a very modern property, with lots of straight lines and glass and all in all it's in very masculine taste. As I move through the living room and into the dining area I notice one of the hard-backed chairs around the table has a split leg, which is bound together with rubber tape. The wooden table itself has a large crack running right across the middle of it, which looks very odd indeed in this well-kept, neat little property. I take a rolled up newspaper from under my arm and place it on the table and by the chair leg in turn, taking pictures that clearly show the newspaper date next to the damaged furniture. Hardly damning evidence, but it helps paint a picture of a household that may have seen some violence.

Behind the table is a large, glass shelving unit with a vase of dried grass placed artistically on the middle shelf. I check the vase to make sure there's no water in it, then carefully remove the grass and fan it out on the table. Onto the central stems I attach my tiny surveillance camera, then roll up the grass and arrange it back in the vase so the camera is facing out into the room. I fit two more cameras before I leave, one in the kitchen, another in the living room, and my stomach turns at the thought of what they're going to record.

When I return to the office, I go straight to Doug's file and take out the memory chip that holds video footage of Anna in a violent rage. I boot up my laptop, insert the chip into the USB converter and load up the scenes of a well-respected female estate agent having a series of violent outbursts. It's car-crash footage, but I have an odd compulsion to watch it. For some reason, I think it might reveal something important to me about Sandra's case.

I buy military issue surveillance equipment, which means everything I film is always very clear and the footage of Anna is no exception. There she is, a beautiful, well-dressed woman with film-star make-up and an immaculate blonde chignon, pulling books from her living room bookshelf and flinging them at her husband, who's doing his best to dodge the best-sellers and restrain his wife before she does him an injury. After almost every book she throws, she smoothes her fitted jacket down around her stomach, which I have to say is bulging slightly over her waistband. It seems out of character somehow – for an immaculate woman like Anna to be carrying extra weight.

Most of the books miss their mark, so Anna decides to do Doug some damage with her hands, by screwing her delicate little fingers into fists and pummelling his chest and shoulders. She's like a madwoman, her face contorted, red and ugly and veins bulging from her pale neck. There are tears running down her cheeks and eventually she collapses on the living room floor, clinging to the arm of the sofa and sobbing. Doug tries to console her, but she flings his arms away and continues to sob into the flocked upholstery.

This is different, *very* different from Sandra's situation, because Doug wasn't scared of Anna – he just wanted to help her. Doug wasn't after divorce footage, he just wanted me to film Anna so he could play it back to her and show her what a monster she had become. And yet I can't help thinking there is a similarity between the two cases somewhere. But what is it?

I pause the footage and take a few deep breaths to calm myself down. This job can be very tough emotionally, and I often think I deserve more holidays than your average employee. It's been over eight months since I worked for Doug, but I decide to give him a call just to check on his progress. I care about all my clients, and I like to see how they're getting along from time to time.

'Doug? It's Mr M.'

'Mr M!' Doug sounds like he's greeting an old school friend. 'Great to hear from you. Just great.'

'How's everything going?'

'Fantastic. Absolutely bloody brilliant. Hiring you was the best thing I ever did.' I can hear Anna singing in the background. 'Anna's carried on with the therapy. That video footage still gives her nightmares, but it did the trick. It shocked her into seeing sense, and something else made her see sense too.'

'Oh?'

'Yes.' Doug sounds ecstatic. 'We've had a baby. A little baby girl.'

'Congratulations,' I say, quite taken aback. 'That was fast work.'

'She's only three months old,' says Doug. 'Her name's Emily.'

I congratulate him again and hang up, feeling really pleased that Doug and Anna are doing so well, but there's something still niggling me. And I can't work out what it is.

As I look at the dismantled parts of my old heater, I have to admit defeat. No amount of hammer blows could get it working this morning, so I took a screwdriver to it instead, forgetting that I'm not, and have never been, a trained electrician or mechanic, and neither do I have a gift for understanding electrical appliances. Now I've taken it apart, I've no idea how to put it back together again and I'm just scooping the pieces into a bin bag when there's a knock at the office door.

'Come in,' I shout, and then wince as I see Sandra poke her head around the door, her cheek clearly swollen and bruised even under several layers of make-up.

'Here, have I seat,' I tell her, jumping to my feet and pushing my wooden office chair towards her. 'Did you bring spare make-up with you?'

She looks confused, but nods.

'We need to get that make-up off your face and take a picture of your injury,' I tell her, ignoring the alarmed look she gives me as she realises just how obvious her swollen cheek is. It's a typical reaction. Because abuse victims are rarely asked outright about their injuries, they assume the make-up and dark glasses really do convince the world that there's nothing wrong with them.

I take the snaps quickly, and I can tell Sandra's ribs are bruised too, by the way she's holding herself, so I ask if I can photograph them. But as I say 'bruised ribs' Sandra looks close to tears, and she clearly finds the idea of revealing the damage to her ribcage too distressing. This is classic abuse-victim behaviour: if nobody looks at it, then it can't be that bad.

'OK,' I tell her. 'With the video footage, we've got everything we need for the police to press charges.' At lunchtime, I collect the surveillance footage from Sandra's house, and am sickened to witness the brutal beating Mark had given her the night before. It had started in the dining room – the scene of most of their rows, apparently. Mark is, according to Sandra, very fussy about his food and a portion of under-buttered mashed potato is enough for him to fly into a rage and start laying into her with his fists.

'Ready to head to the police station?' I ask Sandra.

She nods.

After several hours, Sandra and I have given the police enough evidence to put Mark behind bars. In a few moments, two policemen will escort Sandra to her home, where she'll pick up her belongings, and from there she'll be taken to a woman's refuge. But there's a problem: Sandra refuses to press charges against Mark.

'I just can't do it.' she says. 'Please understand. He's still my husband.'

A policeman nods at me.

'If she doesn't want to, she doesn't want to.' He puts a hand on my shoulder and steers me towards the door. 'But we can take it from here.'

As I leave, the door clicks gently behind me, and so does something in my mind. Anna, Sandra. Sandra, Anna. I see Anna's hands smoothing down the lines of her jacket as she's throwing books at her husband. Over her stomach. Her pregnant stomach. If Doug's daughter is three months old, Anna must have been at least three months pregnant back when I recorded her. Thank God she got help when she did. But Sandra... her arms wrapped around her waist. The way she reacted when I asked about her bruised ribs... the nausea in the café, on the first day I met her... and suddenly, out of the blue, hiring a PI to help her, when she's never sought help before...

Sandra's pregnant.

So that's why she came to me.

But now she just can't bring herself to press charges against her husband, who'll soon be a father. The police can, though. A recent change in the law means police can prosecute a violent husband without the wife pressing charges, and this has doubtless saved the lives of many women too scared, ashamed or confused to press charges against their husbands.

Cases involving domestic violence are never easy. There are so many mixed emotions involved that they're always a mess, one way or another. But the control freak can be defeated once the victim accepts that it is necessary, and twelve months later Mark receives a prison sentence. For Sandra, it's a great relief the police pressed charges instead of her; she couldn't find the strength to see it through to its conclusion but they made the hard decisions for her. Now she and her new baby boy are doing well. She has a restraining order against Mark, and she's filing for divorce.

I don't need to become a bully to defeat a bully. The action I take is fair and proportionate but it's enough to get the job done. I never sacrifice my principles. I won't compromise my morals. Using devious tactics or becoming a bully to achieve my aims negates the pleasure of helping a client and, for me personally, the cost is too high. But still, every year people lose their lives at the hands of someone they love or once loved, so although I stay within the law and my own moral code I am ruthless when seeking the evidence that keeps my clients safe from their abusers.

One of my favourite quotes from an anonymous source is: 'Our destiny is shaped by our thoughts and our actions. We cannot direct the wind but we can adjust the sails.' I hope I've provided a gentle and kind wind to steer Sandra towards the safe future she deserves.

8

A DISHONOURABLE CRIME

Calls from distressed ladies requiring my truth-finding services always cause me concern. But those who advise that they are in mortal danger tend to focus my attention just a little more. The responsibility of a woman's life could easily be overwhelming to some people, but I am always willing to champion the cause. Some of these women see me as a knight in shining armour, but I'm just a businessman with a heart.

How strange it is that a person can walk along a straight and narrow road for the majority of their life, and yet one small deviation can bring with it devastating results, leading to a path from which it is near impossible to return. Most of us are aware of the invisible yet ever-present moral line we know we must not, and yet are sometimes painfully tempted, to cross. In my job I see this so often: lives that are torn apart by the actions and choices of just one individual.

Some people, on the other hand, simply have no choices available to them. They are catapulted into a role set out for them at birth, and the wheels of fate keep turning with little or no input from themselves, even once they reach adulthood. I'm thinking particularly of the Asian clients I have helped over the years, the majority of whom are women. Many Asian women come to me desperate for proof of a husband's infidelity and ill-treatment of them. If an Asian woman chooses to leave her husband she is often ostracised – not only by his family, but also her own. It is simply not acceptable according to her culture, and she is often disowned by the entire family, even if the reason for the end of the marriage is severe and intolerable abuse or worse. These women often beg me to record proof of the severe ill-treatment their husbands subject them to, so they might stand a chance of holding onto the approval of their own family if they seek divorce. But sadly many lose their families if they leave their husband; my heart really goes out to them.

One such woman is Sophia. As is typical of a Muslim girl, Sophia is very reluctant to ask for help and terrified her family will find out and condemn her 'betrayal'. My first contact with her is unconventional to say the least. I'm just ending a phone call with an elderly ex-client of mine who loves to stay in touch and bombard me with local gossip in the belief that she is actually helping me with some of my own cases, a regular Miss Marple – annoying when I'm frantically busy, but very sweet with it. I haven't the heart to end the conversation too quickly as I get the feeling she relishes our chats. I manage to extract myself from the call at the sound of the door knocker, audible to 'Miss Marple' on the other end of the telephone. I say my goodbyes, and as I head for the door realise it's not a caller, but simply the arrival of the morning post. I'm about to return to my desk when I notice a small folded piece of paper. The note is handwritten and the writing is scrawled, and obviously written by someone in a hurry. It says:

Be at the call box on the corner of Acacia Drive and Shawley Avenue, 4 p.m. Tuesday 15th.

Today's date.

My heart begins to quicken in the same way it does during my all too infrequent visits to the gym – shockingly irregular considering it's situated through the door to the right of my office. I have to admit I am a sucker for a good mystery and already I'm intrigued by the contents of the note, if a little suspicious. I have an inkling it's probably a prank; my ex-RAF mates are more than a little partial to the odd practical joke and I'm long overdue a payback. I decide to put the contents of the note to the back of my mind and concentrate on the most urgent tasks of the day. Christmas is approaching and it's my busiest time of year: too many office parties and female colleagues in short skirts, hold-ups and high-heeled boots. I always get a high number of bookings for honeytrappers in the party season. I try to get stuck in, but as late afternoon approaches I find myself donning my overcoat and heading outside into the waiting blizzard. As I said, I'm a sucker for a bit of intrigue.

It's bloody freezing in the phone box. Granted, it's sheltered from the wind and snow, but that's small compensation for the stench of urine flooding my freezing nostrils. I just hope whoever has written the note has good timekeeping. The windows begin to steam up, but I can still make out the figures of other people wandering around outside, heads bent against the inclement weather. I squint in an effort to distinguish faces through the snow, convinced one of my old RAF buddies will pop out from behind a snow-covered bush and drag me to the nearest drinking establishment.

I'm concentrating so hard that the shrill ring of the telephone catches me by surprise. I suck in my breath to steady myself and glance at my watch as I lift the receiver: 4 p.m. on the dot. Practical joke or not, at least their timekeeping is accurate.

I say my name as soon as I lift the receiver, but the voice at the other end is so faint I can barely tell if anyone is there or not. I can hear it's a woman and I hazard a guess she's fairly young, but there's little more I can distinguish. I try to sound reassuring.

'Whatever you tell me will remain in the strictest confidence,' I say. 'It's just you and me.'

I can hear breathing at the other end of the line and thoughts of pranks from ex-colleagues are now far from my mind. Whoever is making contact with me is scared, very scared – and it's no act.

'I need your help.'

'You've got it. I'm here. I'm listening,' I say, in an effort to hurry her along a little. I am here and I am listening, but I'm also bloody cold and some nutter is tapping on the frozen glass to let me know he's waiting to use the phone. I'm tempted to offer him my mobile to get rid of him for a minute, but within seconds decide I'll probably never see it again, so the impatient bugger can wait.

'If anyone finds out I'm doing this I may as well be dead,' she tells me. I can make out an accent and I believe she may be Asian. This gives me a starter for ten: I can anticipate the sort of problems she may be experiencing and it allows me to be a bit more proactive in obtaining the information I need, while reassuring her that she is doing the right thing in contacting me.

I decide to cut to the chase. In all my previous encounters with women in Sophia's situation, one common factor is that they are all convinced they're the first woman in the world to seek help outside of their own family. They're raised to believe that honour is everything and seeking help from outside brings shame on the family. If she dares to speak out against unfair and sometimes brutal treatment, she risks being disowned at best and possibly even abducted or murdered at the other end of the scale. Some families have been known to hire bounty hunters to track down their disobedient daughters and bring them back into the family, often to be locked up against their will.

I can hear muffled sobs at the other end of the line. I pull the collar of my overcoat up around my neck and lean back against the glass, settling myself in for the long haul. It's not going to be easy coaxing the story out of this lady; I guess she's already entrenched in guilt and shame for believing herself worthy of asking for help.

After several more reassurances, Sophia begins to retell some of the trauma she's been living through for the past ten years, and I have to admit it's one of the worst cases of abuse I've come across.

To start with, she married a man ten years her senior ten years ago, when she was just sixteen years of age. The marriage was arranged by her parents and she went along with it entirely to please them, through fear of rejection if she refused. Her mother knew she wanted to go to university to fulfil her dream of becoming a barrister, but told her she would bring shame on the family if she joined wayward westerners in university life.

Within days of the wedding her husband began physically abusing her, slapping her around the face to begin with. He demanded sex whenever he wanted it, without any preamble or regard for her feelings, purely for his own satisfaction and relief. Sex with him was very painful for Sophia as she had fallen victim as a child to a barbaric practice common in her homeland of Iraq – female circumcision. Apparently the practice still exists throughout the Middle East, particularly Saudi Arabia, Jordan and Iraq. Unfortunately it seems that boys growing up in the same culture aren't taken aside in class and told to be gentle with their mutilated future wives. Certainly Chit, her husband, did not listen to her cries and made no effort to be gentle. After a few months together he also subjected her to anal sex without any care to be gentle or use lubrication. When she pleaded with him to stop he would slap her across the face.

Within ten months of their marriage, Sophia became pregnant and with some relief she assumed the abuse would stop. But she was wrong. It grew steadily worse and over the years she barely even bothered to complain about it. The only reprieve was when Chit would disappear for a few days at a time; Sophia never knew where he went and didn't bother to ask for fear of antagonising him.

Over the period of their marriage they had three children together and Sophia began to live through them. She adored being a mother and revelled in the children's unconditional love for her, always grateful that Chit felt the same way; he would never raise a finger to the children and showed them love and concern. She found herself feeling grateful that he would never strike her in their presence; he would always wait until they were in bed, although this led her anxiety to build as the day wore on, knowing what was to come with the arrival of late evening.

Although Sophia hated her life and grew to hate her husband more, she never considered suicide as she knew she must live on for the sake of her children. She thought she had accepted her path in life and bore the abuse for their sake. It was only once her daughter reached the age of six that she found the strength to contact me; her husband informed her that he would be taking the young girl out of the country for a week and she realised instantly what his plan was. He intended to have her circumcised. According to his culture, a female should be circumcised to become a desirable wife and since it is now illegal in this country to carry out this kind of operation, many girls are taken abroad to have the procedure carried out, often without anaesthetic. It is estimated that at least 65,000 women in the UK have undergone some form of female genital mutilation; many of these cases only come to light when the women come to the NHS for maternity care.

As I listen to Sophia I find myself once again stunned that in the twenty-first century women are still being subjected to this kind of torture and abuse and it is condoned by clerics and the like as being beneficial. The female sex drive is so feared that the threat has to be minimised by physical torture. The tradition of FGM is so deeply rooted in the Muslim culture that many men feel revulsion at the thought of uncircumcised women.

Sophia's desperation to protect her daughter from suffering the agony and long-term problems she suffered as a result of her own mutilation gave her strength to finally take action against her husband. But her lioness instinct is only marginally stronger than the fear pulsing through her body, and I can tell by her reluctance to talk to me that she is a very frightened lady.

It's not surprising that Sophia is almost crippled by her own fear; the facts about women in her position make pretty frightening reading. Many Asian women in the UK live in fear of their lives if they attempt to free themselves from the tyranny of male dominance. For some, the only way out is suicide. They can often see no other way. Others simply go missing, vanishing without a trace. A local council report in Bradford a few years ago demonstrated that 150 Asian girls had vanished from the education register. Analysts were tasked with tracking the figures and they pinpointed 1,000 boys and 1,000 girls with Asian names as they moved through school. At primary level, for the 1,000 boys there were 989 girls. At secondary school stage, all of the 1,000 boys could still be found, but the number of girls had dwindled to 860.

'Where have all the girls gone?' was the comment from the senior analyst.

These are frightening statistics, but political correctness and the extreme fear and reluctance of the UK government to intervene in matters when a faith other than Church of England is involved means the problem is swept under the carpet. If the same analyst had uncovered the startling fact that 140 girls had vanished from the education register in a white middle-class Surrey suburb, would not the entire Surrey police force be called in to investigate? Would it not be front page news?

During my conversation with Sophia, I manage to obtain all the details I need to begin working on the case and already I'm hooked. There are cases that ignite a spark in me and this is one of them. I hurriedly gather my notebook, pen and mobile and exit the phone box at speed, but by now it's not the cold making me race. I barely notice the weather as the familiar surge of excitement rises through my ribcage, and adrenaline pumps through my veins. Walking home, I work on my game plan; I love cases that have this kind of effect on me and I can't wait to get started.

My first task is to prepare for an evening's surveillance. I kit myself out with day and night-vision binoculars, my digital video camera and warm clothes – and that's as high-tech as it gets. James Bond-style X-ray glasses don't exist, and even if they did I'd still find a Mars bar more useful during the cold hours I'm sat in my car, observing cheating husbands and crooked employees.

Sophia has provided me with full details of her husband's life: his workplace, his car registration, places he visits and details of friends and family, so I have all I need to start tailing him. She tells me he often doesn't come home until very late, sometimes 3 a.m., and she suspects he may be out with other women, so I plan to follow him when he leaves work, and observe his evening activities.

I find his place of employment easily. Chit works in a typical, anonymous office block just outside central London. It's the sort of place that housed up-and-coming businesses back in the 1970s, but now accommodates the mundane and the unremarkable: companies with bland names like 'EMS Couriers', and 'Investco Trading'.

I've parked up on a side road nearby, out of sight of the tinted office windows, but in a position where I can see cars coming and going into the employee car park. I'd love to say I have a flask of coffee with me, but I think I may be in for a long wait tonight and the last thing I need is to be running out of the car for a toilet break every half-hour.

As it happens I don't have to wait long before I see Chit's grey BMW pull out of the car park, bump over the exit speed bumps and creep onto the main road. As he drives past, I give my indicator a nonchalant flick and pull out after him. I love tailing cars. Maybe it's the hunter instinct in me, or maybe it's because a lot of the targets I follow look better from the back than from the front – who knows. Chit is certainly no oil painting, but then again the back of his head isn't particularly pleasing either. He has a wide skull covered in patchy hair, and small, chubby ears with one sitting an inch or so higher than the other. When I think of Sophia, with her young, frightened voice, I feel nauseated at the thought of this man forcing his sexual attentions onto her.

Chit seems to be heading home, or at least towards the address Sophia gave me as their family residence, but he's going a long way around, almost as though he's purposely taking his time getting there. I'm following him along a typical, affluent suburban street when he suddenly pulls towards the curb and into the drive of a pleasant-looking 1930s property with large, shiny bay windows and a well-kept front garden. It's so sudden I'm thrown for a moment, but I casually drive past the property and pull up round the corner. I can't risk leaving the car in sight of whoever's house this is, or Chit may begin to wonder why my car is following his moves so closely. But I can certainly take my video camera for a leisurely evening stroll to find out more.

I approach the house quick march, one two, one two, straight past Chit's car, and manage to get three shots of the windows as I do so: lounge, kitchen and bedroom. I've already cranked up the zoom, but without looking through the lens and focusing it's hit and miss whether I've got anything useful.

And I haven't. Back at the car, I check the camera to find nothing but blurred shots of kitchen cabinets, an empty bedroom and a blank TV screen – all partially hidden by curtains. Bloody curtains. They'd be number one on my Room 101 list.

I manage to grab a little more 'walk and shoot' footage before I decide I'm beginning to look suspicious, so I bring my car around to a shadowy spot where I can see the house, and wait inside. I drop open the glove compartment and take out my Steiner binoculars. They're perfectly dark, with cone-shaped barrels and purple lenses, and if there are no curtains in the way they can show me things only plastic surgeons should see. It makes me chuckle as I recall that my ex-RAF mates often refer to me as the kinky pervert of the bunch with my binoculars and penchant for night-time stalking, but I assure them that no self-respecting peeping Tom would get a kick out of the things I see! I lift the binoculars but only risk looking through them for seconds at a time, in case someone spots me. Those seconds usually tell me a great deal.

However, right now may be an exception. The kitchen window tells me nothing at all, except that whoever runs the household is very tidy and uses a lot of oil in their cooking. There are litres of it lined up neatly behind the gleaming gas cooker. The bedroom is empty too, but I notice a garish, yellow paisley duvet cover and burgundy flock wallpaper with furry vines climbing all over it. Whose house is it? I'm beginning to doubt Chit's having an affair. What I've seen so far says 'old married couple', not 'unmarried woman who entertains male guests', but if this job has taught me anything it's that you never can tell.

I pan down quickly to the living room and hit the jackpot. The curtains are only partially drawn, and inside the room I see a dead television set reflecting two men in its dark surface. They sit close together on a sofa. One is Chit, and the other has what I consider to be a family resemblance to him, but I could be wrong. Chit is leaning well back into the sofa, one brown-shoed foot propped casually over his knee. He has a whisky tumbler in his hand, and appears animated, seemingly telling some hilarious tale to his companion who suddenly lurches forward, clutching his middle and wiping away tears of laughter. When he pulls himself upright again, I remember something and pull out the notepad I used to jot down the information Sophia gave me over the phone. I scan over my scruffy notes. *45 Juliet Street: Chit's mother and father. 133 Georgia Avenue: Uncle Yusuf.* That's the house I'm looking at – 113 Georgia Avenue.

Uncle Yusuf. I'm disappointed. So Chit and his uncle are enjoying a drink and a joke. Who cares? It's hardly disreputable behaviour. I can't prove what's in that whisky tumbler, and it may as well be tomato juice for all the colour the dark TV screen can show me.

Maybe tonight's not my night. Time crawls forward. By the five-hour mark, it occurs to me that this is what Sophia goes through most nights, waiting until the early hours, never knowing what time her husband will return.

At 1 a.m. I begin to wonder what exactly is wrong with this man who leaves a sweet-natured young wife and two children at home while he stays up all night just a few streets away. I lift my binoculars for the tenth surveillance that hour, but it's all become pretty routine now – the picture never changes. Chit and Yusuf are sitting exactly the same way on the sofa as they did hours before, and by the looks of things are perhaps even enjoying the same joke. But suddenly there is movement. I'm relieved; I was beginning to wonder whether they could go on like this all night.

The front door clicks, and there is the sound of hard shoes on tarmac as the two men leave the house and proceed towards Chit's car. At first, I think Uncle Yusuf must be waving him goodbye, but when both men get in the car I know something else is going on. Within seconds the engine starts up, and they're on the move. I have to play this tail very carefully: it's dark and quiet, and with hardly any cars on the road I can't come anywhere near them without raising their suspicions. It's a case of letting them get as far ahead as I dare and then racing to catch up when they turn a corner, as well as changing from my side-lights to headlights to make it look like a different car is following when the driver next looks in their rear view mirror. As they approach a traffic light, I slow right down and let them pass through the green. The light turns to yellow, but there are no cars around so I cruise through carefully, looking left and right as I do so: not sensible or safe, but necessary for Sophia's sake, or at least that's what I tell myself.

Left, right, left again; gradually I'm losing them in a series of winding streets, and after one more left turn they've disappeared completely. I'm tempted to bash the steering wheel in frustration, but since an airbag blowing up in my face is unlikely to help I drive on and circle the block in the vain hope they've pulled over somewhere. No such luck. It's an interesting area though: I've counted two street walkers and one all-night sauna, so whatever Chit and Uncle Yusuf are up to it's unlikely to be window shopping. More likely they're hunting the late-night wildlife which, if the two girls on the last street corner are anything to go by, is extremely colourful indeed. I turn back onto a narrow street and pull up on the curb. A sign flashes in my rear-view mirror: Pleasures Nightclub, 9 p.m. 'til late. Feeling pretty sure that 'late' means 'gone one-thirty in the morning', I decide it's probably a good place to ask a few questions, and get a drink – for professional purposes only of course. If Chit takes regular late-night drives around this area, someone in the club might know who he is, and who he sees while he's here.

The nightclub has a set of exhaust-fume-stained double doors made of metal and tinted glass, and either side of them are softly illuminated pictures of the girls I'm likely to meet inside. Titania, Honey and Michelle are all waiting for me, pouting and eager, as long as I can afford the ten-pound door fee, thirty pounds a lap dance and at least one drink every hour I'm there.

The reception area is lavish and light, and occupied by a forty-something bleached blonde receptionist who forces a smile when she sees me, and takes my money daintily, like an air hostess removing a used coffee cup. We don't embark on any form of conversation but I get the feeling if I ask for anything I'll get a response along the lines of 'Computer says no'.

I slip discreetly downstairs to the club, and take a seat in the shadows. Strip clubs have never been my thing – probably down to some lingering old-world British gentlemanliness – but I'm happy to pay the girls for their time if they'll answer a few questions. As it happens there's no need. Sitting right in front of the stage, watching a short, curvy and very naked girl walking on her hands along a catwalk-style stage, are Chit and Uncle Yusuf. Chit sits exactly as he did in Yusuf's living room, with one foot propped on his knee, but now he's bouncing his knee up and down. This may be my night after all.

With a few clicks, I turn on my video camera, set it to night vision and rest it on the table. I have to be careful: if management catch me filming, they'll think I'm after a free home movie and kick me out faster than the girls here get their g-strings on and off.

Even in near darkness, I'm sure I'm getting some good footage. Sometimes I think my job is crazy. I can wait around for hours, days even, and get nothing at all. And then I get everything I need within ten minutes.

I leave without buying a drink; I know from experience as soon as you make yourself known in these sorts of places you're suddenly fighting off dancers eager for your cash, and I've had all my questions answered already tonight.

'I didn't think this would be so hard.' Sophia dabs her red eyes with kitchen towel – the nearest thing to tissues I could find for her in my cluttered office – and stares again at the video stills. I've had them enlarged, lightened and printed onto matt paper so she can check the evidence. It has to be irrefutable or she could still risk being disowned, and maybe killed by her family. 'I don't love him. So why does this hurt?' She was almost hysterical when I pulled the pictures out, sobbing so hard I thought the neighbours might come running. It's not an uncommon reaction. As much as some wives are aware of how their men behave when they're out of sight, seeing it in black and white is a different story.

'Of course it's hard,' I tell her. I want to say, 'I have no idea why a man with a beautiful woman like you would pay to visit a strip club.' And she really is beautiful. But I catch myself and say instead, 'You deserve respect from your husband. I understand why this would hurt.'

Sophia sighs – a lovely, clear sigh, and she gives me a soft smile.

'Now we have something on him,' she says, and leans her head on my shoulder. I'm a little disquieted by this sudden gesture of familiarity, but then again I'm the first person in years to look out for her. It's no wonder she feels safe with me. It makes me even more determined not to let her down.

'But it's not enough. My family… his family… they might say it isn't him.' She leans closer into my shoulder, and I feel her soft hair on my cheek. 'Can you get more?'

'Of course I can.'

I couldn't have refused, even if I'd wanted to.

Later on in the week Sophia visits my office in a state of nervous excitement: her husband has left suddenly for a weekend away. She asks if I can keep her company while she checks his home computer for any evidence that may help her. As the computer is her property as well as his I agree to sit with her, for moral support as much as anything else.

We take my car. The drive towards Sophia's home is mostly silent but I'm aware that she's staring at me from the passenger seat. The intensity of it is a little unsettling, and I try to focus on the road ahead.

'Why do you do what you do?' she asks eventually, her large eyes still fixed on my face.

I ponder her question for a moment and consider why, in the midst of this crisis in her life, she should be showing such an interest in my own motivations.

'Sometimes I don't know why,' I answer truthfully, 'but at times like this I realise it's because I want to help people.' I glance across and gaze for a moment into her dark eyes. 'People like you,' I finish, instantly regretting the words. Often, when clients are experiencing severe problems in their lives they turn to me for comfort and I try to remain professional, but friendly. When the client involved is an attractive and intelligent woman like Sophia, it's not always easy to keep that distance, although I believe it is essential if I'm to remain professional and do the job to the best of my ability.

Sophia seems to be happy with my reply and the hint of a smile brushes her lips. She looks even more beautiful that way. I slow to a stop as Sophia's house comes into view: a Victorian detached property in a sought-after Surrey suburb. Clearly money is one thing Sophia doesn't have to worry about. I release the central locking and we both get out and walk into the house.

I sip a cup of coffee as Sophia starts up the family computer, and she shows me a number of password-protected documents that she has tried to access without success. She sets to work with a password decrypter she bought from me and within ten minutes at the click of the mouse a folder pops up entitled 'Chit Private'.

Inside the folder I find some JPEG image files and word documents. I feel Sophia's excitement rising with my own as she asks what we should look at first. My instinct leads me to click on a JPEG file, and I'm immediately shocked as an image of a naked Sophia fills the screen in front of us.

'My God,' I hear Sophia whisper as my face fills with colour. I click on the X to get rid of the image and turn to the horrified and embarrassed girl in front of me. I feel so deeply for her, I want to shield her from further embarrassment, so I rise to leave.

'No, please, Mr Martinez, stay,' she pleads.

I open some more JPEG files, many of them pornographic in nature, and heavy enough to shock even me. Some of them feature people I don't know and others are clearly images and video clips of what Sophia once thought were private moments between herself and her husband. As the images flash before us I become aware of Sophia's leg close to my own and I shift in my seat to create some distance between us.

Then I feel her hand over mine.

'It's all right,' she says. 'I know this is embarrassing for you too.'

'You know he shouldn't be able to do this?' I ask. 'You know that, don't you? Marriage is no excuse.'

Sophia sighs. 'I wish my family thought like that. But... I think they'd say if a husband wants to photograph his wife, then that is all right. As long as he isn't selling the photographs or showing them to anyone else.'

Her hand is still covering mine.

'Sophia, can you show me the bedroom?' I ask.

'Of course,' she says. She doesn't sound surprised or offended.

'He must have a video camera hidden in your room,' I say. 'That's how he's getting these pictures. They're film stills, not camera shots. That's why some are blurry.'

She shows me her bedroom, and it's as bare as I imagined with only a small, plain double bed and a functional wardrobe as furnishing, and no pictures or ornaments. There's no love in this room. It's as sterile as I'm sure her marriage must feel.

I spot the camera straight away – it's a knack I've developed over the years, almost a sixth sense; when you spend as much time watching others as I have you know when you're being watched. It's a small device fitted with a battery pack and set facing the bed. A red light tells me it's running.

'It must be filming twenty-four/seven,' I tell her. 'It's lucky you're a faithful wife.' I begin to unhook the camera.

'What are you doing?' says Sophia, alarmed.

'I have to delete footage of the two of us coming into the room together,' I tell her. 'Don't worry – I'll make sure he can't tell anything is different.'

'Somehow I knew he'd done something like this,' says Sophia softly. 'I tried not to think about it, but I've always had this eerie feeling I was being watched.' She shudders visibly. Maybe she subconsciously knew it was there all along. It's amazing how people can adapt to control. Denial is a strong religion in many unhappy marriages.

It's 11 p.m. and I'm in my study uploading video footage onto my laptop. For three weeks, I've been following Chit and learned the visit to Pleasures Nightclub wasn't a one-off. There are several lap-dancing clubs he visits, and one of them, Desire, is a well-known pick-up club for men who want more than just a lap dance.

I click open film files and scan through to find the Oscar-winning moments: Chit waving notes at a topless blonde dancer, Chit drinking from a beer bottle while Uncle Yusuf enjoys a lap dance and Chit disappearing into a dark stairway with a nearly naked brunette. And I've got something else on camera besides visits to strip clubs. Or rather someone else. A girl. She's a twenty-something brunette who works as a receptionist at Chit's office complex, and she has an unusually expensive selection of clothing for someone of her age and occupation. Every Wednesday and Friday lunchtime, Chit drives her to a nearby block of high-rise flats, into which they disappear for half an hour or so, before reappearing and driving back to the office. It doesn't surprise me that Chit is living out the cliché of an affair with a girl from the office: he's fulfilled so many male chauvinist stereotypes I'm amazed he doesn't have stuffed stag heads hanging in his living room.

I've got some good shots of Chit and the office girl driving together, but I need to film them going into the block of flats if

Sophia is to convince her family that Chit is behaving badly. So far I haven't managed it. The tower block entrance is on a pedestrian-only road, and it's been too risky to park up and run out of the car to film them. I need to be waiting, discreetly, when they arrive.

Generally, though, I'm happy with how things are progressing. I'm about to pour myself a celebratory nightcap when my mobile phone rings. The sound tinkles at first, then gets louder and louder. The number is from a BT payphone, and I have an uneasy feeling. A very uneasy feeling.

When I put the phone to my ear, all I can hear is uncontrollable sobbing. My stomach feels tight and sick. It's Sophia.

'Please...' she manages to say through the tears. 'You can't work with me any more. He knows.'

Out of the corner of my eye, video surveillance is still running on the laptop. I can see Chit swigging a beer and pushing a twenty-pound note into a dancer's hand.

'Sophia. Listen. Are you OK? Did he hurt you?'

The sobs tell me all I need to know.

'Where are you? I'm coming to get you.'

'No!' She practically screams the word. 'No, there's no way. He'll kill me.'

I'm finding it difficult to hold the phone. But although the thought of Sophia standing in a cold phone box beaten and scared is awful, I am sure that Chit has done something very stupid.

'Where did it happen?'

'He said...' Sophia ignores my question, takes a few deep breaths, and sounds calmer. 'He said he felt someone was watching him tonight. And that if I ever watched him he'd kill me.'

Relief floods through every cell in my body.

'I wasn't watching him tonight,' I say. 'Listen, Sophia, I haven't watched him since yesterday. But where did it happen?'

She breaks down again.

'He came home furious,' she says through her sobs. 'I was pretending to sleep, but… he grabbed my hair and threw me out of the bed. I was screaming at him, "What? What have I done?" He kept punching me and punching me. In my ribs.'

What a coward. Even in a rage, he made sure he beat her where nobody could see.

'I think he beat me more because I sounded guilty,' Sophia says. 'Because I was…' She pauses. A long, poignant pause. '… thinking about you.' She takes another deep breath, and so do I. Then she says, 'Maybe this isn't a good idea any more.'

'Sophia, I know you're scared, and if you want to call this whole thing off, we can,' I tell her. 'But he's just given us one more nail in his coffin tonight. There's a film camera in your bedroom. And it's filming twenty-four/seven. It will have recorded Chit beating you, and I can take the recording and copy it. We can show your family. And it's Friday tomorrow. Tomorrow I'm planning to get all the evidence you need to show your family what kind of husband he is.'

'Friday? What's so important about Friday?' she asks.

I don't tell her about the girl at the office. If I can't get the evidence I need, I don't want to hurt her dignity even more by telling her about the affair.

Instead I say, 'Will you give me one more day? Just one more?'

'I don't know.'

'Please, Sophia. One more day.'

A pause.

'OK. But that's it. I'm too frightened to go on.'

I have to get film footage of Chit and the girl going into the flat tomorrow. I have to. Or all Sophia has hired me for is one more beating.

Thank God it's Friday. I'm waiting on the pedestrian path by the high-rise block of flats, pretending to stand and smoke a cigarette, while discreetly holding my camera at the entrance. People come and go, and no one pays me much attention, especially not the portly Asian man and the young, dark-haired girl who walk briskly into the building. As the security door swings shut behind them, I stroll past the entrance, point the camera inside and without breaking my step head to my car. I've got all I need.

Sophia and I watch the footage of Chit and the other woman, his arm around her skinny shoulders guiding her into the building when he thinks they're out of public view.

She holds my hand tightly, but she doesn't cry. There's a feeling of hope, like the time she first rang me, hope that she may be able to escape this awful prison that has been built around her.

We've decided I won't go with her when she shows her family the evidence. It's something I'm not happy about, but Sophia knows her family well and she thinks it won't be for the best if she takes a strange man along to meet them.

It's 10 p.m. and the air in my apartment feels dry, close and oppressive. I can't keep my eyes off the phone, even though I know sitting looking at it isn't helping my state of mind. I care about all my clients and of course Sophia's no different, but there's something so vulnerable about her. It's knotting up my insides to think of what she's going through. She must be so frightened. I told her to ring me at 9.30 p.m. to let me know she's OK. Chit won't let her have a mobile, so the only way I could contact her is to drive around to the family homes she's visiting – which she's expressly forbidden me from doing.

The clock on my mobile phone has just flicked up another minute. When it reads 10.02 p.m. I'm calling the police.

Suddenly there's a familiar tinkle, and my phone lights up. I grab it.

'Sophia?'

'Mr Martinez.'

She sounds... OK. The relief is absolute.

'What happened?'

She tells me the whole story. First she visited Chit's family, and they were outraged. Her dreams of total acceptance and understanding from a caring mother and father-in-law were instantly shattered. At first they accused her of falsifying the video footage, but as each new example was presented they became more contrite. Eventually they told her she was trying to bring shame on the family and threw her out.

She ran to her parent's home, where there were tears and raised voices, but her family were angry with Chit and themselves, not with her. And they told her they'd support her. They'd help her seek a divorce and let her and the children live with them in the family home. It was more than she could ever have hoped for.

'Thank you, Mr Martinez.' I can feel the waves of love and gratitude down the phone line. 'I can have a life now. You've given that to me. I'm safe. I have a life.'

As we say our goodbyes, it occurs to me that chance led Sophia to me, but that she also led herself there. She decided, for the sake of her daughter, not to let the wheel of fate roll along as she had before, but to try and steer it in another direction. A better direction. And she finally has a chance at happiness.

9

A HONEYTRAP AND A SECOND HONEYMOON

Picture the scene – it's an uncomfortable summer's afternoon, blazing hot sunshine tempered by very little breeze. Your heels sink into the beautifully manicured lawn belonging to the managing director of your husband's company and your dress, the one your husband insisted you wear, clings to your body in all the wrong places. You shift self-consciously and stand with one leg slightly in front of the other in an attempt to hide the tell-tale streaks of badly applied fake tan you resorted to earlier. Having resigned yourself to an obligatory attendance at the firm's annual barbecue with as much relish as an anticipated trip to the dentist, you try to look as if you're enjoying yourself, smiling as people pass and exchanging small talk with anyone who stops long enough on their way to the free bar in the middle of the lawn.

You feel slightly uneasy since you know very few of your husband's colleagues well enough to exchange more than the briefest of conversations with and he, forgetting your earlier request that he stay nearby until you 'warm up', is too busy mingling somewhere between the water fountain and oriental pagoda gazebo to notice you are standing alone with an empty wine glass in your hand.

In the distance your attention is caught by a young woman who seems to be staring at you. She has a drop-dead gorgeous figure, barely contained within her casual jeans and strapless clingy top. Her large breasts sway slightly as she walks and suddenly you feel overdressed. Clearly she feels a bra is surplus to requirements on such a white-hot afternoon, and anyway, she doesn't need a bra; 250 grams of silicone appears to doing the job unaided. As she makes her way in your direction, you examine her with intensity and to your embarrassment she does the same to you. You glance, first over one shoulder and then the other, to see whether she is heading determinedly for someone behind you. Puzzlement replaces scrutiny as her stare does not waver. You are definitely her target. She moves towards you with confident ease. Despite her silver sandals with stiletto heels she glides across the lawn, her fake smile marginally more impressive than her obviously fake boobs. Not wanting to appear unfriendly you edge towards her, bobbing up and down like a demented penguin as your heels sink further into the vandalised lawn, leaving several divots in their wake.

'Hello, you must be Mrs Osborne?'

Her perfect olive complexion is complimented by flawless 'no make-up' make-up, her fresh face free from any trace of perspiration, despite the soaring temperature. As you nod and take her proffered hand you notice her beautifully manicured fingernails and make a mental note to stop chewing your own.

'I'm Kelly and I'm going to marry your husband.'

Everything stops. Like a DVD that freezes mid-frame. You look for the hint of a smile in her porcelain doll-like face but her plump lips remain set in a line of defiance, no hint of amusement in her piercing blue eyes. You stare at the young woman and she stares back, her face serene and without a trace of embarrassment, as if she'd just commented on how well the roses seemed to be doing this year. In slow motion the garden begins to reform, its colour and shape replacing the obtrusive comments swimming around in your mind. You force a laugh, hoping it will be infectious, desperate for her to slap her sickeningly slender thigh and shout, 'Gotcha!', your husband, ever the practical joker, heading over to put his arm around you and smile at her conspiratorially.

'Very funny. You almost had me for a moment.' You force another laugh in the hope of putting an end to the unwanted exchange.

'I'm not joking. I'm in love with him. It's only a matter of time before he's mine.'

'Don't be ridiculous.' You snap at her, surprised by the sudden ferocity in your voice. You wish she'd take her toned backside and crimson fingernails and disappear into oblivion. In an instant you feel foolish, trying to convince yourself once again that the woman who stands opposite, or perhaps you should call her a girl since she is at least ten years your junior, is merely one of your husband's colleagues with great acting skills who has been sent over to wind you up.

Relishing the look of bewilderment on your face she pauses for a moment then turns abruptly, leaving with a final defiant smile in your direction and sashaying off in the direction of your husband, her equally defiant bottom wiggling seductively in the over-tight jeans. You remain rooted to the spot, your mind racing almost as rapidly as your pulse. It has to be some sort of a joke set up by your husband. Surely this young woman wouldn't be brazen enough to make such an outrageous announcement if she really wanted him?

It may sound like fiction, but I listen attentively as I sit on Carol Osborne's sofa and she recounts the events of last summer.

'It was when I told him that I knew I had a problem.' Carol constantly runs her fingers through her greying hair as she talks, revealing the inner tension she feels. I wait for her to continue but suddenly she seems lost for words.

'You think they're having an affair? If that's the case I can find out for sure. All I need is...'

'No, no, it's not that,' she interrupts, shaking her head. 'She's dead. It's definitely not that.'

Now I'm confused. During our earlier phone call Carol told me she was worried about her husband but several cups of tea and home-made Madeira cake later and I'm still none the wiser. A beautiful girl announces her intention to marry Carol's husband and now she's dead. I feel like I've walked onto the set of *Desperate Housewives*, or 'desperate housewives with overactive imaginations'.

Now I'm the one rubbing my head. 'I'm sorry, Carol, but I'm confused.'

'He was pleased you see, when I told him. I could see it in his eyes, a sort of roguish glint. I should never have told him what she'd said. He was so flattered. Sure, he tried to hide it, but I knew. He laughed when I got upset about it, told me how much he loved me and said it didn't matter what Kelly said, he could never be interested in anyone else.'

'But you didn't believe him?'

'Of course not, she was gorgeous,' she speaks sullenly. 'And he's so handsome, he looks like Robert Redford, in his younger days, you know. I'm just a frump.'

I open my mouth to object but she waves her hand, dismissing my unspoken reassurances.

'But now she's dead?' I try to move the conversation forward a little to get some idea of why I'm here. I find myself hoping she's not about to make a confession that she bumped off the competition and needs help to hide the evidence.

'Yes and I feel so guilty about it.' She begins to cry. This is it, I begin to panic; I'm going to be asked to dispose of the body she has stored in the chest freezer.

'What have you done, Carol?'

'I wished her dead, on the day of the barbecue I wanted her wiped from the face of the earth. And from then on, the knowledge that David spent each day at the office in her company instead of with me made me wish her dead. Six days after the barbecue she was killed in a crash on the M25.'

Carol hangs her head and for the first time since my arrival I believe every word she has said. As I organise my thoughts and continue to puzzle over why I'm here she blows her nose and raises her head to meet my gaze, her eyes swollen and skin blotchy.

'I know it sounds awful but I felt so relieved when David told me the news. I knew she was right, you see. It would have been just a matter of time until he fell for her, and I love him so much.' She begins to cry again and I feel for her, not only because she is so upset but also because she suffers from the widespread female affliction of self-loathing and lack of confidence. She's an attractive woman, despite the flecks of grey snaking languorously through her honey-blonde hair. Although I'm fascinated by her story, I still have no idea why she is telling me all of this.

'I'm sorry. Shall I make you another cup of tea?' I've already sussed the entire layout of her kitchen having made the last two rounds.

To my disappointment she nods vigorously, blowing her nose with equal vigour. The last thing I need is more tea but I know from my study of human psychology that people are most at ease when you mirror their actions. I want her to relax and get to the crux of the matter.

Halfway through my fifth cup and the penny finally drops. Carol no longer trusts her husband to resist the charms of a sexy woman if she shows an interest in him. She has convinced herself that his flattered response to the news that Kelly wanted him is evidence he would leave her at the drop of a hat if the opportunity arises again.

It's 8 p.m. and I abandon my motorbike in the rear car park of the Brixton Windmill, venue to a variety of acts. David, it turns out, is a man after my own heart, a bit of a rocker. Tonight the Windmill are hosting a new band going by the name of Self Destruction and as I make my way through the entrance I find myself surrounded by a sea of fans in almost indistinguishable outfits of black. Ever the master of disguise I am sporting a wig of shiny black locks with a middle parting, black T-shirt and tight black trousers; de rigueur for any self-respecting heavy rock fan.

Unfortunately my disguise is not cunning enough to fool Barry, a regular at this establishment.

'Richard, how are you, mate?!' He slaps me on the back as high as he can reach. Barry stands at five feet six and suffers from chronic small man's syndrome.

'Is there something going down tonight?' His face looks up into mine eagerly, excited by the prospect of a 'case' unfolding before his piggy eyes.

'Barry, belt up!'

'Copy, mate, copy.' He gives me a conspiratorial wink as I turn abruptly and head for the bar. Unfortunately Barry discovered my profession a couple of years ago following a conversation with one of my mates from the football club who'd had one too many sherberts, and he can't resist mentioning it despite my lengthy explanations of the need for discretion.

It's been four weeks since my tea-fuelled afternoon with Carol and this is the first opportunity I've had to arrange a honeytrap, since David doesn't often go out in the evening. This suggests to me he is a man perfectly content with the company of his wife, but nothing other than hard evidence is going to convince her otherwise, so here we are on a brisk evening in April, me looking like the clone of Frankenstein, and Cara, one of my most attractive honeytrappers, looking very fetching in short black low cut dress with shiny silver high-heeled sandals.

I hardly recognise her at first. Cara is a natural blonde but the woman standing at the opposite end of the bar has raven-black hair. She catches my eye for a moment then removes a lipstick from her handbag and reapplies a layer of pink gloss across her lips. Carol was very specific in her requirements for this evening, almost obsessive. She wanted a woman who looked just like Kelly to try and seduce her husband. She had to have large breasts, long black hair, olive skin, fingernails painted red and a tight little bottom. Cara was my nearest match; she bought a wig similar to the one I'm wearing and she made up for the shortfall in chest measurement with several of her husband's socks tucked into her bra. Her outfit may not be one of a classic rocker but it fits my client's brief and at least it's black.

I know David is here; I noticed his Ford Mondeo parked up a few streets away. We both spot him at the same time. Cara watches as he leaves the gents and makes his way over to the bar then returns her gaze to her compact. He stands just a few feet away from me and I have to admit, Carol described him well; his yellow-blond hair falls casually across his forehead and he stands with a self-assuredness of someone who, in stark contrast to his wife, is entirely comfortable in his own skin. His square chin and bright blue eyes complete the look, although I'd say he falls short of the charms of Robert Redford, but then I'm not his wife.

Unaware of my attention, David responds to Cara's friendly smile from across the bar. She turns away then and appears to be people-watching as more rockers flow through the doors like black crows gliding over to order their drinks. David picks up his beer and makes his way over to Cara on the other side of the bar, no doubt drawn by her inexorable power. My view of her is partially blocked as he stands close to her, like a viper swallowing its prey, I think wryly, feeling sad for Carol who waits anxiously at home, praying her husband will pass the test she has set for him.

I watch them talking and record every moment with a discreet video camera hidden inside the collar of my black casual shirt.

As he turns sideways I notice he appears relaxed and happy to be talking to Cara. Even from this distance I can make out a roguish sparkle in his blue eyes. Suddenly they throw their heads back in unison, no doubt in response to some witty story Cara has relayed. She runs her fingers through her long shiny hair, pushing it back from her face. He smiles warmly, undoubtedly enjoying her company.

Ten minutes later and the act is about to begin. As everyone makes their way to the auditorium David lowers his head towards Cara, whispering something into her ear. She nods in acknowledgement. That's it then. He's fallen hook, line and sinker. My heart sinks. I had high hopes for David. Carol told me that apart from her insecurity they enjoyed a blissfully happy marriage.

'And you can't break up a happy marriage, can you, Richard?' She had asked me earnestly, a hopeful look on her face.

'No, I don't think you can,' was my answer, though as I watch the pair across the bar holding each other's gaze and raising their glasses in a silent toast I don't feel quite so sure.

'I'm so happy, Richard. Thank you so much.' Carol throws her arms around me, delighted by the news I've come to give her.

'You've got nothing to thank me for. I'm just pleased you're happy.'

'I am, so happy. And so relieved. I can put a whole lot of demons to bed now and just enjoy my life.' A single tear runs down her cheek and she hugs me again. She doesn't ask to see any of the footage from last night and I don't feel the need to show her. All she needs to know is whether David has passed the test and, to his credit, he has. I have no doubt he was attracted to Cara but he left it at that. He chatted to her for a while and then left her alone, making no effort to get her number or pursue her any further. He left the venue at the end of the evening and went home to his anxious wife and I couldn't be happier for her.

Three cups of tea later I finally manage to extricate myself from her friendly hugs and leave her planning a second honeymoon as a surprise for her husband.

Three weeks later and I'm back at the Windmill but tonight it's purely a social visit. Septic Shock are playing this evening and I've come along with a few of the lads from my football team.

'Another sucker fell for her then?' I bump into Barry at the bar and don't move quickly enough to escape conversation.

'What's that? What sucker?' I ask absently, uninterested.

'You know, that blond bloke, the fucking Robert Redford lookalike she was working her charms on a few weeks ago.'

'No, he didn't actually,' I answer almost defensively, subconsciously shifting my body away from Barry. I feel uncomfortable discussing work issues with someone entirely unrelated to the case and I'm eager to draw this particular conversation to a close.

'Oh right, he didn't manage to track her down then?' Barry, with as much sensitivity as a brick, fails to pick up on my hostile body language and plods on regardless. ''Cause he seemed pretty desperate to find her.'

My curiosity pricked, I drop the bored look. 'What?'

Barry senses my interest and appears delighted to be telling me something I don't know, as if he's suddenly morphed into Hercule Poirot. 'The next day. He came back the next day, asking around, trying to find out who she was. Asking where he could find her…'

While the others lose themselves in sounds of distorted guitars and double bass drums I go over and over my conversation with Barry, trying to decide whether I should tell Carol the news. I was employed to test the strength of her husband's loyalty; withholding information from her could be described as unethical. And yet she had welcomed the news with such relief it would almost be cruel to shatter the illusion.

I arrive home after 2 a.m. and crash out on the sofa, too exhausted to make my way into the bedroom. I wait for sleep to overcome me but I know it's going to be a difficult night. I lay, listening to the symphony of rain outside the window and the ticking clock on my mantelpiece, wrestling with my conscience, but after two hours of thrashing the thoughts around in my mind I'm still unable to reach a decision as to whether to reveal the truth to Carol or not. My neck begins to ache. I roll over and reach for my mobile to check the time. It's 4 a.m. Two hours of debating over the obligations and moral issues involved in concealing the truth from someone who has placed their trust in you and I'm still no nearer a solution. I decide it's time to take positive action. I fling my phone back down onto the sheepskin rug and make my way into the kitchen, hoping a bacon sandwich can clear my mind.

Sadly, delicious though it is, my early morning breakfast doesn't offer the epiphany I was banking on. Feeling like the only person this side of the earth not sleeping I stare fixedly at the kitchen clock. My pre-dawn vigil ends when my head slumps forward onto the breakfast bar.

I wake as the first dim shades of yellow dance their way through the slats of my kitchen blinds. I blink several times, surveying the scene without moving my head. I have one hell of a stiff neck. It's 9 a.m. when I finally reach the decision to pass the information to my client. I feel she has a right to know and besides, not telling her would probably only be delaying the inevitable. David's pursuit of Cara, though it came too late for him to find her, speaks volumes about his willingness to cheat on his wife.

'Hi Carol, its Richard.' My stomach begins to turn over and it's nothing to do with the bacon sandwich.

'Richard! How lovely to hear from you. How are you?'

'I'm good, thanks.' Guilt washes over me as I anticipate spoiling her day; she sounds so chirpy. I allow myself a moment's reprieve by asking her how she is.

'Brilliant, thanks. Things are better than ever. I'm so much more relaxed now. David has noticed the change I think. He's no longer living with a stressed-out nutter!' She laughs loudly. 'You're lucky you caught me actually. We're flying off to the Maldives this afternoon, you know, for our second honeymoon. David was so surprised when I told him I'd arranged it. And it's all thanks to you, Richard.'

My body relaxes a little, the acid in my stomach obediently returning to a normal level. There's no way I can tell her now. I say my goodbyes, explaining the reason for my call as a general follow-up, a customer satisfaction survey of sorts. I replace the receiver, ashamed of my cowardice. How could I tell her, after hearing the happiness in her voice? It is perfectly possible, I try to convince myself, that David won't hurt her in the future. And maybe the old saying, 'What the eye doesn't see the heart doesn't grieve over' has a nugget of wisdom in it. Carol paid me for some peace of mind and that's what she got. Only time will tell whether that peace is to be shattered.

And after all, had I not returned to the Windmill so soon after the honeytrap I may never have had the conversation with Barry and I would probably be as Carol is now, in blissful ignorance. I try not to analyse the vagaries of fate too deeply; if the summer breeze had been a touch stronger this time last year Kelly may have joined the motorway a second or two later than she did and may have lived a long and happy life. It may have been a long and happy life with Carol's husband, but who knows? That's the way life is.

10

SECRETS OF THE BOARDROOM

West London. It's lightly drizzling as I drive along Arlington Street and park my car outside the main entrance doors of the Ritz Hotel a few minutes before 11 a.m. It feels odd to be abandoning my car in the middle of central London, but it's definitely something I could get used to. As soon as I open the door and step out of my car I'm greeted by a rather camp-looking concierge, immaculately dressed in a heavy blue-wool coat and a sergeant major's hat decorated with gold piping.

I introduce myself, unnecessarily as it happens.

'Yes, Mr Martinez, Mr Moss is expecting you, sir. Would you like to give your keys to Tony? He'll take care of your car. Please, come this way, sir.'

I follow the concierge as he minces through the foyer and into a bar area, where my new client, Mr Moss, rises from his armchair seat and walks towards me, his hand outstretched. He's wearing a tailored, wool suit and a bright-pink tie.

'Mr Martinez, sir.' The concierge announces my arrival rather grandly and then discreetly departs, backing away with a slight nod of his head in my direction.

'Call me Richard, please.' I take Mr Moss's hand and shake it.

'Richard, shall we pop downstairs for a coffee? It's quieter down there during the day. And by the way, call me John.'

John leads the way through the foyer, down a set of stairs and into a magnificent room of red and gold. It's stunning in size and décor. All lighting is indirect and softly falls on paintings and exquisite furnishings full of colour, and yet tastefully elegant. The ceilings are high and the room, which must be forty-foot long, has windows running the length of it. It's been a few years since I last visited the Ritz – my girlfriend at the time splashed out on a champagne dinner as a birthday celebration – but I've never visited the Ritz Club before. This place is something else. I feel a little incongruous in my run-of-the-mill off-the-shelf suit with no accoutrements of style. What I need is a tux.

John heads for an armchair tucked away in a recess and I take the sofa opposite. Within seconds of my bottom touching the seat we're approached by a waiter who takes our order for two coffees. As the waiter sweeps away soundlessly, almost gliding across the red and gold carpet, John leans forward and speaks in a low tone.

'Richard, firstly I apologise for being so vague earlier, but what I have to tell you is not ideal for discussing over the phone. My company is in trouble and I suspect it may have something to do with my business partners – I need you to find out what's going on.'

'What makes you think it's in trouble?'

'We're losing business, it's as simple as that, and it has nothing to do with the credit crunch. Our cash flow is shot to pieces and a fortnight ago we lost one of our biggest contracts to a rival company. Six months ago we were thriving, despite the country being in the throes of a recession; we were doing really well.'

'Why do you suspect your partners?'

'I've always enjoyed a good relationship with Ken and William, despite being the new boy on the block – they brought me in as a director six years ago. We've always got on well, personally and professionally. But around six months ago things began to change: whispered conversations between the pair of them, sudden silences when I walked into their office unannounced. It's no coincidence, Richard. I can sense it: I know something's going on. I've tried discussing the business problems with them but they just don't seem interested. It's as if they don't even care what happens – the answer could be they're fleecing me in some way. I can't let that happen; that's why I invited you here.'

John falls silent and waits for me to respond.

'If I'm to get to the root of the problem quickly I need to be in on the inside. I need to work for you.'

'Excellent!' John looks happy for the first time. 'The timing couldn't be more perfect in that case – we're holding interviews tomorrow for a vacant post and I've done all the paper sifting so I can slip an application from you into the pile without raising suspicion.'

Our coffee arrives and I spend the next twenty minutes or so taking notes from John. Only then does he reveal the name of his company: a hugely successful, multimillion-pound organisation dealing in electrical and computer technology. I'll refer to the company as Glenco to protect anonymity.

Back at the office I get to work on my fake curriculum vitae, inventing an enviable sales career beginning as a sales assistant at the tender age of sixteen and working my way up to sales manager of a small team at an anonymous-sounding company. I'm banking on the fact that most companies neglect to carry out decent checks on potential employees – a naive way to operate, but it happens all the time. We are a trusting nation on the whole. Directors of companies spend a fortune on building an IT fortress, ignoring the greatest threat there could ever be to security: rogue employees. Even cleaners and ancillary staff, anyone with access to the office, should be vetted and references checked. I believe the going rate in London at the moment to task a cleaner to steal information from their employer is twenty pounds. It can take them seconds to steal or use their mobile phone to photograph a vital document, or even use the company photocopier to take a copy.

Two recent studies show that insiders are responsible for more than 70 per cent of information-related thefts. As I told John earlier, it's so easy to access and copy information from the inside, like taking candy from a baby. I have found most company directors assume information security is computer security, but this is not the case. While computer security is an integral part of a good security programme, it's only a part. Comprehensive security includes physical, operational, technical and most importantly, personnel security. Industrial spies know how to bypass any strong part of a security programme to attack an organisation at its weakest point: from the inside.

British companies lose millions of pounds annually due to industrial espionage. The threat prevented by firewalls is minimal. A rogue employee with limited knowledge can bypass the strongest protection mechanisms and pass vital information on to a competitor. The galloping pace of technology means eavesdropping and theft of information is becoming a growing problem for companies.

Rivals can easily get hold of a colourful array of sophisticated gadgets to spy and steal business; mobile phones and the Internet make it even simpler. Electronic bugs can be enclosed in an apparently normal mobile phone battery, creating a listening device that is able to transmit the user's two-way conversation.

Take my last case, for example. My client was the director of a very successful, national PR company. He called me in when he suspected foul play of some sort. One of my first checks was to sweep his offices for bugs. All was clear until I checked his office and my detector picked up a bug in his pocket – he reached in, handed me his mobile phone and sure enough, there it lay. It appeared innocent enough and yet it had allowed an unscrupulous rival to listen in on all his business and intimate conversations. Of course, I couldn't find out how long it had been there, but it could have been months. I always advise my clients to record the file number on their mobile phone battery. Most people never bother to do it, but when millions of pounds are at stake and crucial business secrets need to be guarded it's a sensible safeguard.

It's often assumed that industrial espionage is stuff of fiction, but that's not the case. It's very real and rife in all avenues of business. In 2001, Procter and Gamble admitted spying on their rivals, Unilever, for secrets of their shampoo. Boeing was punished by the US Air Force in 2003 for resorting to espionage in order to better its defence rival Lockheed Martin.

According to The Institute of Directors (IoD), the potential of becoming a victim of industrial espionage now seems to be bigger than ever. I certainly have experienced an ever-increasing number of calls from anxious company directors suspecting espionage in some form or another. I regularly sweep companies for bugs and when I find them people are horrified. According to estimates, more than £10 million-worth of bugging devices have so far been sold in the UK; that's an awful lot of bugs. I suspect many are lurking inside boardrooms or under desks where critical business plans are discussed.

Turning a blind eye to the problem is not an option. Many companies will use a variety of methods, some legal, some grey, and some clearly in violation of the law, to obtain trade secrets. All managers and directors should prioritise security of information if they want to protect their business. As Bernard Esambert, a President of the Pasteur Institute, once said, 'Today's economic competition is global. The conquest of markets and technologies has replaced former territorial and colonial conquests. We are living in a state of world economic war and this is not just a military metaphor... the companies are training the armies. In a tight market, information is vital and especially in cases of mergers or hostile takeovers. A leak somewhere can make the difference between failure or success.'

It's the morning of the interview and I'm struggling to rouse myself. I slept like a log last night and my muscles have that glorious liquid feeling that having too much sleep can give: a rare luxury for me. It's late October and the leaves are rapidly falling from the trees in clusters of red and gold. I neglected to close the curtains last night and the morning sun is bright, flooding my bedroom with light, and yet the chill in here tells me the temperature will barely hit ten degrees by lunchtime. I'm reluctant to leave my bed. Despite the fact it's a sham interview, nerves are getting the better of me – I know John would choose me of course, but it was already arranged that Ken would conduct the interview. And there are seven other applicants. If I don't get the job I've blown my cover and that's not something I want to happen. When I take on a client I like to see the job through to the end and I've never failed yet.

The grey-haired receptionist smiles at me as I push through the glass doors and head towards her desk.

'Laurence Brown,' I tell her, smiling easily. 'I'm here for the interview.'

'Take a seat on the sofa, Mr Brown. I'll let Ken know you've arrived.'

She gestures to a firm leather sofa between her desk and the lift, and I take a seat, picking up a glossy IT magazine from the glass coffee table as I do so. As I casually flick through the pages, I'm feeling confident – cocky even. I know I look the part and my CV is outstanding. Studies suggest interviews are more about personality checking and CV verification than proof of skills, so as long as I remember the details on my CV and present myself as calm and amiable, I stand a good chance.

As I'm turning pages, marvelling at how any magazine could be so boring, the lift doors slide open and a man and woman step into reception. The woman is very tall and slim, and dressed in a fitted, black trouser suit and high heels. Her bobbed haircut is cut so sharp it could cut sandwiches.

'Thank you so much for your time,' the woman says, shaking the man's hand. 'And thanks for seeing me to the door, too, I know you're busy.' She's smiling, and with her ultra-slender body dressed in black from head to toe, she looks like a very happy Biro.

'No problem.' The man looks tired, but he manages to drag a smile onto his grey face in response to the woman's enthusiasm.

She's still smiling. Her cheeks must be in agony.

The woman sashays through reception and through the glass doors to the street, and the man abruptly turns to me.

'Laurence?'

It's so spur of the moment, I almost forget my new name.

'Er... yep. Hello. That's me.'

I stand up and shake the man's hand.

'I'm Ken,' he says. 'I'll be conducting your interview today.'

'Great. Nice to meet you, Ken.'

He seems too exhausted to reply. As I follow him into the lift, I try for some friendly small talk.

'Beautiful weather we've been having, isn't it? Almost a bit too perfect for autumn.'

Ken doesn't reply. In fact, he remains lost in thought until we're sitting opposite each other in the interview room, and he's laid my CV in front of him. I use the opportunity to size him up, taking in his manner, clothing and general energy.

I'm guessing Ken is at least mid-fifties, maybe older. His face sags with tiredness and a thick, permanent worry line runs across his forehead. He blinks slowly, reminding me of an owl.

'Why do you want to work for us?'

'Because Glenco is a well-established company with a good reputation and I know I would feel confident selling your products. I have to believe in a product to sell it.'

'How do you know we have a good reputation?'

'I know you started the business over twenty-five years ago and since then you've grown to become one of the leading suppliers in the country. I also read that you and your partner, William I believe, both left school at sixteen and worked seven days a week on a market stall in Brixton market until you had enough money saved to rent your own shop.'

'I'm impressed, Laurence, you've obviously done a bit of detective work.' He sips at his tea and eyes me suspiciously, or maybe I'm being too paranoid. Perhaps it's because I like to be the one asking the questions.

'What do you do when you're not working, Laurence? Any special interests?'

'I like to dabble in a bit of photography.'

I leave feeling pretty confident I've made a good impression; most people thrive on someone showing a bit of interest in them and I'd done enough research on the partners (pretty easy when I had John to fill me in on anything that would be in the public domain) to give the impression I found Ken a bit of an inspiration. I'm pretty sure he looked a lot brighter when I left the office than he had following Ms Biro's departure. Having been in many situations where I've needed my wits about me, I trust my instincts more than some people might. But I must confess that the smiling lady has unsettled me. She was very dynamic and confident, and, despite his weary farewell, maybe Ken was as impressed by her as I appeared to be by him.

'Congratulations, Richard, you've got the job.'

John tells me it was a unanimous decision, although Ken was swaying towards the girl in the smart suit.

John opens the door and offers his hand. 'I hope you have some luck, Richard.'

'I make my own luck.'

He nods and smiles broadly, revealing shiny white teeth, the product of an affluent childhood or cosmetic dentistry.

'I can believe that.'

The next day I'm pushing through the glass doors again, but this time the receptionist greets me by name and welcomes me to my new place of employment.

'Thanks. That's really kind of you,' I tell her. 'Where should I go?'

She taps a pen on the reception desk and frowns.

'Ken should be here to take you up and show you around,' she says. 'I don't know where he is. I suppose you'd better just go on up to the sales floor. Take the lift. Floor three.'

I thank her, but decide to use the stairs instead. That way I can get a little stair-aerobics after an hour stuck in rush-hour traffic.

In contrast to the plush, heated reception area, the stairwell is cold, dusty and devoid of soft furnishings. A grey-metal staircase leads right up to the top of the building, with little metal platforms on each floor and draughty, aluminium-framed windows lining the wall. I take the stairs two at a time – *clang, clang, clang* – noting the plywood doors leading to each floor as I make my ascent.

On the third floor, I'm about to leave the stairwell when there's a bang below me as a door swings open. I hear men's voices. Angry men's voices.

'For God's sake, look at you, man. You can barely keep your eyes open, let alone manage a team of people.'

'Keep your voice down,' the other voice hisses. It's Ken's voice – I'm quite sure. 'Who else can I ask? Tell me that. Who?'

'Listen to yourself. Think about what you're asking. John knows something isn't right, Ken. What if he finds out? Does he have the burden of it, too?'

'There's no one else.'

There's a silence. Then the first man says, 'Just think about what you're asking.'

I hear the door open and the two men leave the stairwell.

I wait for a moment, digesting what I've just heard. Ken is in some sort of trouble, there's no doubt about that.

On the third floor, a team of around ten sales reps are barking down telephone lines, assuming various dominant-male postures. Some are leaning back with their hands behind their heads, and one or two have their designer-leather-shoed feet up on the desks. I can smell the aftershave immediately, a combination of various expensive fragrances, and notice the glimmer of diamond-encrusted watches and signet rings. There are no women here, which is perhaps why Ken was keen to take on a female sales rep: the atmosphere is savagely male and pulsating with testosterone.

At the far end of the room, a huge whiteboard is screwed to the wall, scrawled with marker pen. Names are written on the left: Darren, Paul, Simon, and so on, while the right side lists their sales leads. Kevin has by far the most sales leads – ten this week – and I wonder which of these predatory creatures he is. Then I spot him: a hair-gelled, baby-faced lad sitting in the corner, scratching his head with a pen and holding a mug that says 'Kevin'. There's also a Garfield on his desk holding a heart that says 'Kevin', so I'm fairly certain it's him. Either that, or Darren is having an identity crisis.

Since Kevin is the only person in the room not on the phone, I head on over and introduce myself.

'Nice to meet you, mate,' says Kevin, leaping to his feet and grasping my hand with enthusiasm. 'What can I do you for?' He's throwing my hand up and down with some vigour.

'I'm the new boy,' I tell him, looking around the office, trying to work out where I'll be sitting. 'Got the job yesterday.'

'New boy, eh?' Kevin's eyes light up. 'Great. Great, mate. Let's get you started then. Take a seat.' He gestures to the desk next to him, and begins to explain Glenco's products and services. He finishes by saying, 'Basically, mate, you've got a good product, and a load of f-ing idiots, 'scuse my French, out there with a lot of money to spend.'

He plonks himself down in his chair, picks up the phone and dials a number.

'Hello? Mr Hamish? Yes, hello, Mr Hamish. It's Kevin from Glenco. Now I've got some good news for you today...'

As I listen to Kevin's sales patter, I realise he's expecting me to start making a few phone calls. He's left a lead sheet in front of me with various business phone numbers, so I pick up the phone and start ringing around. I've never sold so much as a sausage roll before, so this should be interesting.

By lunchtime, I've made three leads – more than anyone else in the office – and I'm beginning to think maybe I'm in the wrong career. It turns out, if you're a genuine sort of bloke, selling is easy. Don't promise the moon, listen to people, rather than talk at them, and that's it. By lead number three, I notice the sales team have all angled themselves so they can listen in on my calls, like a bunch of hyenas swarming around a lone antelope, but I don't mind. Maybe I can teach them a thing or two.

By the third morning at Glenco, the nine-to-five lifestyle is taking its toll. I've had enough of early starts, rush-hour traffic, time cards and dry sandwiches from the work canteen, and I've certainly had enough of Kevin and the rest of the sales team. Since the working day is so tightly monitored, detective work is proving much more difficult than I anticipated, but this morning I aim to break free from the sales floor and get a proper look around.

'Kevin, mate?' I lean back in my chair and tap Kevin on the shoulder. 'I need to have a word with Ken about my employment contract. Can I have ten minutes?'

Kevin nods distractedly, as he crosses off names on his lead sheet.

Ten minutes. I intend to make the best of it. I've already been told Ken's office is on the first floor, so I head down the stairwell and quietly enter a corridor lined with, I'm presuming, managers' offices. I read the names on the doors: William Hudson, Ken Bartlett and then my client's title, John Moss. I'm tempted to knock on the door and say hello, but I'm distracted by loud voices coming from William's office.

'... Wait... going home...'

The voices are muffled, but it's definitely two men. And once again, I'm sure one of them is Ken.

'Letters... there's no way... it's over.'

Suddenly, the voice I take to be Ken's becomes very loud.

'For God's sake, William! Don't you think I've suffered enough?'

There are more murmurs, and then suddenly the door flies open and I'm standing face to face with Ken, who looks... well, devastated. It takes him a moment to register that I'm there, and then to recognise who I am. He looks guiltily at the door behind him.

'Did you...? Never mind. What are you doing here?' His eyes are red and watery as he waits for my explanation.

'I wanted to ask about my contract,' I lie smoothly. 'Kevin said you were free.'

'Did he now?' Ken looks very suspicious. 'Laurence? You're Laurence, aren't you?'

I nod.

'Well, Laurence.' He says my name as though it has a bad taste to it. 'I think I might like a word with you in John's office.'

'OK.' I stay calm, but my gut tells me this isn't good. Maybe he wants to go over contracts with John in the same room, but I doubt it. Something tells me I'm a naughty boy about to be led to the headmaster's office.

Ken knocks on John's door, then opens it without waiting for a response. As we enter, John is leaning back in his executive chair and studying a thick sheaf of paper. He looks up, and when he sees me his eyes register alarm – just for second. Then he casually takes a sip of coffee.

'Can I help you, Ken?'

'You tell me. Is this him?'

'Who?'

'Him. Your personal Sherlock Holmes.'

John and I look at each other, then he sighs and rubs his temples with his thumb and forefinger.

'Yes, Ken. This is him. His name is Richard Martinez. He's been taking a look around the place.'

I decide it's time I said something.

'Excuse me. John? Perhaps we should have a discussion in private. I'm not entirely sure what's going on here, and I think maybe you need to bring me up to speed.'

John holds up his hands.

'It's OK, Richard. I told Ken and William this morning that I'd hired a PI. I thought it about time we were all straight with each other.'

Nice of him to tell me. I feel like a prize idiot.

'So what happens now?' I ask, noticing Ken is breathing heavily. He's put a hand to his chest and is making wheezy noises.

John shrugs. 'Carry on with the detective work. Obviously, we'll have to drop the charade of you working here. But I'm sure you have other ways of getting information.'

Ken staggers forwards suddenly, and places a heavy hand on John's desk. His eyes are swimming in and out of focus.

'Ken?' John leaps to his feet, but Ken waves him away with his free hand.

'I'm OK, OK,' he wheezes, taking deep breaths. Then he pulls himself upright and his eyes come back into focus, although his face still has that grey, haggard look.

'Richard...' he turns to me. 'Time for you to go.'

After a tedious afternoon of desk research, I'm no closer to uncovering what's going on at Glenco and now the two people most likely to have some answers, Ken and William, know who I am and what I'm up to.

I decide tomorrow night I'll sweep the office for bugs and check the computer system to see if any suspicious files or copies have been made recently. But before that, I'm determined to speak with William face to face. Ken is a closed book, I'm quite sure of that, but William might be a different story. With the right questions, he might crack and tell me what's going on. There's no time like the present, so I ring his private number, listed on the employee data CD John has given me.

'Hudson.' William's voice is curt and no nonsense.

'Hello, Mr Hudson, sir. It's Richard Martinez here – the private detective John has hired.' I have a whole speech prepared, but surprisingly William is very agreeable to an interview and asks me to come over.

I fit myself with a bug and hit the road. The adhesive tape holding the tiny transmitter at the small of my back chafes a little as I mount my motorbike and kick the engine into life. It's the least hairy place I could find in a hurry, but I can tell I've caught a few stragglers. It's at times like this I wish I was more like the blokes on the cover of *Men's Health*, not so much as a follicle in sight. Still, I'd rather tolerate a bit of chafing than subject myself to the horror of a back, sack and crack.

Within half an hour, I've parked outside William's modern apartment block in Canary Wharf. I look up in wonder at the sparkling glass and great beams of metal that create the dynamic modern-art housing structure. Quite something, if you like living on the set of the Jetsons.

William shows me into his modern living room, with floor-to-ceiling windows overlooking the Millennium Dome. I take a seat on a white-leather sofa and William sits opposite.

'Mr Hudson, you've had several heated discussions with Mr Bartlett in the past few days. Can you tell me the nature of those discussions?'

William sighs and closes his eyes. When he opens them I expect to see anger, but instead he appears humiliated. He still does not respond.

'I'm so sorry to ask you this, sir, but I really must insist.'

He shakes his head and looks away. 'I'm afraid I can't help you any further, Richard.'

I get the feeling from his point of view this conversation has gone way over the line of acceptability already. When he next meets my gaze it's clear he views me with disgust – or disappointment, at the very least. I stare at the carpet.

I feel embarrassed to insist at this point, but the option to walk away when things get nasty is not written into the PI job description; this is simply one of those tasks I have to grit my teeth and get on with.

When I look up his eyes lock into mine.

'Are you going to give me an answer, sir?'

He gives a non-committal shrug and I read his defiant expression as, There are some things we must accept but not understand.

'I'm not going to answer that particular question, Laurence, I mean Richard, or whoever you are today.'

'Then I have no option but to dig further into your life until I come up with the answer myself.'

'All I can do is ask you to accept my word as a gentleman that you're on the wrong track, Richard. My discussions with Ken have nothing whatever to do with the problems at Glenco, trust me.'

'I'm afraid, with the situation as it is, sir, your word as a gentleman is not enough.'

William looks up at the ceiling in exasperation, but remains tight-lipped. I'm running out of ideas; I simply don't know how to spur him into revealing what clearly is a very personal matter. It occurs to me he may be having a homosexual relationship with Ken and fears I'll spill the beans to his wife. I know they've been married for nearly thirty years. It's unusual for me not to figure out a way to get to the truth somehow, and talking to people is something I'm good at. Some people are naturally intuitive, but for those who aren't, it can be learned through practice – I've always had a knack of making people feel at ease and I've had a lot of practice too, so I don't often struggle. But William is proving a tough cookie. I decide to appeal to his sense of fair play.

'Mr Hudson, I dislike intently having to ask a man of your stature such intrusive questions. I appreciate your need for privacy. However, I have been employed to carry out a task and I have no choice but to continue until I achieve a satisfactory result. I assure you, if what you tell me has no detrimental bearing on Glenco it will remain in the strictest confidence. You have my word, sir.'

His deep sigh conveys his contempt for my contradiction, asking him to accept my word but refusing his own.

'OK, OK, but if you want to prevent more prying just tell me this. Are you and Mr Bartlett lovers, sir?'

William throws his head back and bellows in response to my question. It's not a forced laugh, he appears genuinely amused. I can't help but respond with an embarrassed half-smile, half-grimace. Now I've asked it, the question seems ludicrous, and it's certainly clear William thinks so.

'Nothing of the kind, my dear boy, no. You couldn't be more off-track, I promise you. Now I think it's time you left.'

I'm ushered into the hall, William still chuckling as he follows me to the door. But I don't give up that easily. One more thought occurs to me. I turn to face him and look him straight in the eye.

'Mr Bartlett is in trouble, isn't he.' It's a statement, not a question, and William nods, almost instinctively.

'Does he owe money? Is he using you to try and sort out debts of some sort?'

He blows air from his cheeks.

'Why don't you tell me? You seem to have all the ideas, Mr Martinez.'

'Well, I do know you and he are good friends. I know you are highly thought of by your colleagues. If an old friend asks you for help I get the feeling you'd find it hard to turn your back on them, I can gather that much.'

William shakes his head, all trace of humour gone from his face now.

'Ken has enough problems, Mr Martinez, believe me, more than enough, but none of them financial.'

'If the talks were about friendship, why were you arguing?'

'If I tell you that I'll probably end up in prison one day and I can't risk that. I have my family to think about.'

Filled with frustration, feeling I'm nearing the truth but not as quickly as I'd like to be, I reach behind me, put my hand down the back of my trousers and rip the transmitter from my back. Smarting from the pain of having a mini-back wax in the presence of another man I drop the equipment into William's hands.

'It's just you and me.'

William gawps at me for a moment, before taking my arm and leading me back into the sitting room. He takes a long breath and walks to the window.

'Ken wants me to murder him.'

The shock of his confession floors me for a moment. I say nothing, continuing to stare at his back as he stands looking out of the window.

'I'm afraid I don't understand.'

'He is ill Richard, terminally ill. There's no hope of recovery and the prognosis is dire to say the least. He is in constant pain already. He's trying to carry on 'business as usual' but it's only a matter of time before he'll be unable to walk, incontinent and all the rest of it – he can't face it. I'm his oldest friend and two months ago he asked me to help him die with dignity. That's what we're arguing about. I've told him he is wrong to ask that of me. How can I murder my best friend?'

He raises his hand to his forehead as if to communicate the ineffable sorrow inside. He attempts to say more, but his voice fails him and he turns to face the window once more. Ashamed for the second time this evening and a little lost for words myself, I let the silence overtake us for a moment.

'I'm sorry, Mr Hudson.'

'It's all right. I suppose you're just doing your job. Just give me your word you won't repeat a word of this conversation. Ken isn't ready to tell anyone about this yet. I'd say we have to respect that, wouldn't you?'

'Yes, absolutely. You have my word, I'll tell no one. But there are big problems at Glenco, sir, and with your permission I'd like to continue with my investigation.'

William nods in my direction. I'm about to leave when another thought occurs to me.

'Just one more thing, sir.' I return to the living room, kicking myself for sounding a little too like Columbo and hoping William hasn't made the connection.

'How many new employees has Glenco taken on in the past six months?'

William shrugs.

'I really couldn't say. Four or five? Staff at the lower levels tend to turn over quite quickly.'

'Thank you. Thank you very much.'

Email to: All Glenco Staff
Subject: IT maintenance tonight: 6.30 pm
At 6.30 p.m. tonight the building will be closed for routine IT maintenance. All personnel are required to leave this building by this time. Thank you for your cooperation.

The IT maintenance is, of course, a smokescreen for yours truly to have a proper look around the Glenco offices, sweep for bugs and install hacker-resistant IT security. I've already checked every phone, mobile phone and laptop for listening devices and found nothing. But I'm convinced I'm missing something. I believe William's story about Ken, but I also believe John is right to be suspicious about the company's sliding profits. I'm pretty sure there's something going on here that's just not cricket, so I'm on the deserted sales floor deciding how I'm going to check every staff member's computer.

I'm just considering getting myself a plastic-tasting coffee from the vending machine, when I hear a rustling sound. It's coming from inside the stationery cupboard at the other end of the office, so I creep to the opposite end of the room and hide under a desk.

After a minute or so, there's a creaking sound and a peroxide-blonde girl with long hair extensions emerges from the stationery cupboard. She looks around in a theatrical way, like a heroine in a horror movie, then creeps nearer and nearer to where I'm hiding. The next moment, she's sat on a swivel chair just inches away and turns on a computer. She's so close I can see the long ladder in her beige stockings and the blotchy white-and-red skin underneath. Pinned to her skirt is a Glenco swipe card holder with her company photo ID inside. There's a terrible pixelated photo of her on the ID, looking washed out and peaky, with the name 'Annette Wilde' printed above it in blocky black letters.

She has a patent-leather handbag with her, and from it she takes a memory stick coated in black rubber and inserts it into the computer. After a few beeps and clicks, the memory stick is dropped back into her handbag and she tiptoes out of the office, looking all around her as she does so.

As soon as the door closes, I struggle to my feet and quietly follow her out of the building.

Annette is a dream to follow. She's an erratic and highly stressed driver and barely notices traffic lights and zebra crossings, let alone anyone on her tail. As I watch her indicate the wrong way and plough through red lights I realise she's driving directly to the headquarters of Glenco's chief competitors, AGS. No roundabout route to throw me off the scent – no, she's headed straight there.

AGS is based in a highly secure building just outside London, surrounded by green fields and woodlands. As I watch Annette disappear through the main security gates, I know I haven't a hope in hell of getting into the building, so instead I wait in the company car park and set up my telescopic camera. There's a single privet hedge, about the height of a chair, between the car park and the security fence, and since there's nothing else in the empty car park that I can hide behind, I decide I'll have to make do with it as a cover. I'm about as well concealed as a bald head under a comb-over, and I probably look more conspicuous pressed up against this hedge than just standing in the car park taking pictures. But I conceal myself as best I can and point my camera at Annette as she enters the building.

She disappears from view, but soon an office light flickers on and I see her appear on the third floor with a tall forty-something gentleman wearing a beige suit. The two kiss passionately, and after five minutes or so I'm beginning to wonder if they'll ever break apart. But they do, and Annette hands the man the memory stick. I take picture after picture, and have just taken a good close up of the man's face when I hear a sound in the distance: the clattering sound of shoes on tarmac.

'Oi!'

Two tubby security guards run towards me, both panting with the exertion. It's too late to make a run for it. I look at the hedge, thinking it's the most useless bit of cover I've ever hidden behind, and decide they have me banged to rights. Fancy that. Caught twice in one day. I'll never live it down.

The security guards are just a few metres away now, and I really can't think of a good reason as to why I'm pressed up against a privet hedge with a camera in my hand.

'Listen, mate,' one of them shouts, breathing hard to get his breath back. 'You can't go for a piss here, it's private property. Can't you find a pub or something?'

'Er... all right,' I shout back, thinking any minute now they're going to see my camera. Then inspiration hits me.

'I've, er... I've got me old fella stuck, lads. It's stuck in my fly. Give us a minute, would you?'

They both turn and grin at each other, stopping in their tracks.

'Happens to the best of us, mate,' shouts one. 'Cor, I bet your eyes are watering, aren't they?'

'Just clear off when you're done,' says the other. They turn and leave. I wait a moment or two, then jump on my bike and zoom off as fast as my wheels can carry me. I chuckle to myself as I think, 'A dick in the hand is worth two photos in the bush!'

'That's Peter Caraway,' says John, as I show him the pictures. 'I have no idea who the girl is. She works here, you say?'

'Either that, or she's got hold of an ID card from somewhere.'

'Impossible,' says John. 'No – she must be an employee.' He shakes his head. 'You read about this sort of thing, but... this is unbelievable. I think I was happier when I thought Ken and William were up to no good.'

'And Peter Caraway is?'

'AGS's head of marketing. I've met him at IT conferences before. Terribly overbearing fellow. He must be getting information on our ad campaigns and marketing initiatives. No wonder it's been an uphill struggle these past few months.'

'I'm guessing he and Annette have some sort of relationship,' I say.

'It wouldn't surprise me,' says John, leafing through the photos again and looking closely at the shot where Peter and Annette are kissing. 'She looks young and naive, and he's known as a bit of a ladies' man.' He puts down the photos.

'So. Are you going to tell me what's going on with Ken and William, or are you still determined the two of them should remain a glorious mystery?'

I smile.

'I'm not going to break a promise,' I tell him. 'But as I said, it's nothing the company needs to worry about. You'll probably find out soon enough, anyway.'

John nods, and I'm glad he's decent enough not to probe any further.

'I suppose the next step is to get the police involved,' he says, dropping the photos into his briefcase and snapping the locks shut. 'Who'd have thought?' He shakes his head again. 'Industrial espionage. You see it in films, but you never imagine it would happen at your company. Well, thank you, Mr Martinez. I think you've just won the "employee of the month" award.'

The situation at Glenco probably won't be solved overnight, and John has a long road ahead, littered with potential problems. But now at least he knows one of the biggest threats to his business. And I'm confident he'll be grilling potential employees thoroughly in any future interviews he conducts.

11

BAD NANNY

It's 9 p.m. and I'm getting dressed for a night on the town. My date for this evening is an attractive redhead ten years my junior and I'm going smart especially for the occasion; her husband-to-be tells me she loves men suited and booted so I have to look the part if I'm to put a little temptation her way. Little does she know, her night out with the girls this evening involves, perhaps, one of the most crucial tests of her life. Pass and she'll get to keep the biggest engagement ring this side of the river (Andy tells me he almost needed to remortgage to buy it). Fail and she'll be waving goodbye to more than a large diamond; the future she thinks awaits her may belong to someone else.

I know a fair bit about the lady in question already. Her name is Lena, and Andy, her fiancé, tells me she has a love of horses and she's a real rock chick – her favourite band being Deep Purple. This is a stroke of luck; I don't need to do any research in that department since I have every album ever released by Purple sitting on a shelf below AC/DC and above Metallica back at the office. Apparently she's partial to a great chat-up line too – I guess that's one of the reasons Andy is going ahead with a test of her loyalty. She may love a bit of attention, but will she give me the brush-off before it goes too far?

'You're a very attractive man, David, what are you doing wasting your time on me?'

I'm sitting opposite Lena at one of the round tables near the stage where Electric Savage have their Marshall amps notched up to eleven. Fearing my ears are hovering dangerously on the verge of bleeding, I suggest we move over to a table nearer the window – our conversation so far has been a series of screams over the rock music, and hurried chats between songs as the front man interacts badly with the audience; it's obvious he fancies himself as a bit of a comedian – dropping punch lines and then pausing just that bit too long to await the bellows of laughter that don't quite materialise. Clearly the clientele here prefer his musical talents to his humour.

If you're wondering where 'here' is, let me fill you in. I'm in the infamous Half Moon pub in Putney: a live music venue which has played host to the Rolling Stones, The Who and U2 in the past. In short, genuine rock royalty. The band on stage are less like royalty and more like the pack of corgis that snap at the queen's heels.

I arrived about an hour ago, and immediately located Lena at the bar, which is usually the first place I check for a target. I ordered a drink and stood across the bar from her in a position that allowed me to keep her in my sight and yet not reveal myself as paying her any attention at all. For the first forty minutes or so she remained in deep conversation with a blonde woman wearing glasses and a particularly bright shade of red lipstick, her attention wavering only to respond to the intermittent texts she received, three in total.

I note the time of the texts out of habit; I'm here to perform a honeytrap but if I can add some extra information in my report to Andy I am happy to do so, and, after all, if it's not Andy sending the texts, who is his fiancée receiving messages from late on a Saturday evening? It could be innocent; I'll let Andy decide.

The arrival of the interval offers me my first chance of the evening to approach Lena, as the members of Electric Savage abandon their equipment and head for refreshment at the bar. Her blonde companion, having not come up for air since I arrived, heads for the ladies, her black oversized handbag tucked rather undaintily under her arm, no doubt intending to add another generous layer of crimson to her already thickly coated lips.

'Great sound, eh?' I offer in Lena's direction. Not one of my best chat-up lines, but I've found it's generally the delivery of the line and the confidence it portrays rather than the verbal content that's the make or break in terms of pulling.

'Absolutely, one of the best I've seen lately, though I think he should stick to singing,' Lena laughs and gestures to the stool recently occupied by England's answer to Marlene Dietrich.

Across the pub, I notice Lena's blonde friend being accosted by a skinny man with a ponytail as she returns from the toilet. The man is obviously trying to chat her up, but she doesn't seem unhappy about it, and starts chattering away to him.

'Yes, love the music,' I continue, 'though it doesn't quite compare to Purple.'

'You're a Purple fan?'

'Does the pope wear a funny hat?'

She laughs again in response to my rather lame attempt at humour and I can tell I've broken through the initial barrier almost everyone presents to the world. We spend the next thirty minutes extolling the virtues of Richie Blackmore versus Steve Morse, the current lead guitarist with Purple. And now she asks me why I'm wasting my time talking to her.

'Why do you say that? Wasting my time? I'm spending my evening talking to a beautiful woman. I can think of worse ways to spend my time.'

'But you must have spotted my ring, so you know I'm engaged to someone – you're not going to get laid are you? You could spend three hours chatting to me and go home on your own. Are you telling me you're not bothered?'

'Of course, it's not all about bumping and grinding is it?'

She eyes me suspiciously.

'Maybe not, but I think most men would think so.'

'Is that what your fiancé thinks? Is that why you're out without him?'

She considers my question for a moment and shakes her head.

'Two years ago I would have said no but now, now I think it's different. Why am I telling you all this anyway? I feel like I'm on a date with my shrink.'

'I love telling complete strangers my innermost problems,' I say. 'It's cathartic. You can walk away at the end of the night and leave all your crap behind, and all for the cost of a pint! I do it all the time.'

Lena giggles girlishly.

'In that case, let me get you another – what's it to be?'

I've been on orange juice all evening so I let her order me a pint of Fosters and a packet of salted peanuts.

'Why is it different now then?'

A sad look crosses her eyes and she stares at the table for a moment.

'It's my fault, I've ruined our relationship – when I met Andy he was the perfect man and I changed him. Now all I want is the old Andy back, but it's too late for that.'

'But I thought you said I was wasting my time, as if you didn't want anyone else?'

'I did. I don't want anyone else ever again. I love Andy, but I ruined our chance of happiness and now he wants someone else.'

I spend a minute or two sipping my beer and trying to get my head around what's going on here. I have Andy paying good money, £300 to be precise, for another man to chat up his fiancée because he's scared she may prefer a stranger to him and now Lena is dripping involuntary tears into her wine glass and worrying her fiancé wants someone else. Maybe Andy is after evidence of disloyalty so he can wriggle out of an engagement he regrets?

Lena throws her head back and downs the rest of her drink in one, giving me a cheeky smile as she bangs her glass down on the table and moves to refill it quickly.

'So, David, what's the best sex you've ever had?'

I'm shocked for a second or two by the bluntness of her question.

'Why do you ask?'

'I'm your co-shrink remember, you can tell me anything, and besides, the answer to every facet of our personality is tied up with sex, isn't that what they say?'

'Well, as a matter of fact I'm not a particular follower of Sigmund Freud but I like talking about sex as much as the next man.'

'And?'

'The best sex? Well, I suppose the most uninhibited sex would have to be with women who have been slightly... what's the word... unhinged, I would say.'

'What do you mean?'

'I've known some intense women, unreasonably jealous, or if not jealous then driven, hungrier than your average person and that translates into unrestrained sex with no limits where it feels the possibilities are endless, do you know what I mean?' I check I'm not shocking her by my frankness, but she's nodding and smiling and she hasn't poured her drink over my head yet so I continue. 'I think it's true that some of the best sex takes place in the context of love, but it depends on the person you're in love with. If there are psychological limits on either side the experience will be less intense.'

Lena has turned to face me full-on, staring at me with new eyes.

'Please go on, I'm fascinated.'

'It's all about discovery I think; a willingness to cross boundaries, not just in your body but with your mind. Pure physical pleasure can be achieved with a stranger, if you make an immediate connection, but great sex involves the whole psyche; erotic bliss is at the place where love, lust and respect collide – a joining of souls. You can't love and respect a stranger can you? However erotic and unrestrained the experience there will always be something missing. That's what I figure anyway; would you agree?'

When I look back at Lena she has tears streaming down her face and I'm worried I've offended her by going too far.

'I'm sorry,' I burble, handing her a tissue and feeling foolish for responding far too honestly.

'No, it's all right, honestly, it's not you, I just…'

A constant thrumming vibrates the floor, courtesy of Electric Savage, as it all comes out: the reason she's in tears and the motivation behind her fiancé paying me to spend the evening with the woman he lives with. I have to admit it's one of the more unusual stories I've heard in a while, even in the circles I mix in.

Lena tells me she first met Andy when he was eighteen and still a virgin. Lena was twenty and a bit of a man-eater even then, but she knew on their first meeting that he was 'the one'. Despite the feeling he was a little intimidated by her overt sexuality he excited her in a way she'd never felt before. And besides, he had many more attractive qualities; she found him to be intelligent, caring and open, and he possessed an exuberance, a love of life she found infectious and enchanting. Andy obviously felt the same way about her: he proposed within six weeks of their first meeting and she accepted without hesitation. All sound a bit too perfect?

You're right, oh cynical reader, there was just one snag. A little snag that grew into one big carbuncle. Following their engagement, Lena, despite growing to love Andy deeply, found herself unable to face the prospect of sex with only one man for the rest of her life. Being an open book she explained her feelings to Andy. Why did they have to be monogamous just because society says that's the way to be? She told him she didn't want to go round having sex with loads of men, but she just couldn't get rid of the feeling she wanted something more.

Andy seemed shocked at first, shocked and hurt, no doubt his pride wounded by the fear he couldn't satisfy his partner. Lena went for therapy, searching for a reason, perhaps some unhappy memories from childhood, to explain her irrational longings, but after six months of soul-searching she decided to stop questioning herself and start questioning the norm. Having had space and time to let things sink in, Andy began to get used to the idea of other sexual possibilities and after entertaining the idea through bedroom fantasy the couple agreed to embark on an exploration of new sexual avenues together.

They made contact with other, like-minded couples and soon after they began to have sex with other people with full knowledge, consent and, more often than not, participation of all four. Lena tells me she fell in love with Andy all over again as she watched him with other women. Seeing him through the eyes of other lustful women fuelled her own desire for him and filled their sex life with new inspiration. It was intensely satisfying for both of them.

About six months later they met another couple around their own age, Lisa and Martin. The attraction between them was instant. In the beginning it was purely sexual, as it had been with all the others, but pretty soon Lisa and Andy formed a deeper bond based on many common interests and a similar dry sense of humour. On meeting up they began to pair off and rather than noises of bumping and grinding, Martin and Lena could hear raucous laughter and non-stop chattering filtering through the walls of the bedroom. This was far more disturbing to their partners than the moans and cries of passionate sex.

In their previous trysts, the couples would often join up and spend their time in the same room; part of the thrill was to watch their partner having sex with someone else in their presence. Occasionally they would swap round or one partner would observe a threesome in action, but when Lena invited Lisa to join her so Andy and Martin could watch, both Andy and Lisa refused. For the first time in the relationship Lena began to feel jealous. It was as if Lisa was usurping her exclusive right to monopolise Andy's emotions. Lena had always been the liberal one, with Andy following her lead, but now the tables had turned and she became increasingly uneasy. Unable to rationalise her jealousy, she became more needy and craved constant reassurance from Andy.

Lena suggested they split from Martin and Lisa and move on to find a new couple. When Andy showed reluctance she became wild with jealousy, threatening to cancel their engagement and end their relationship. Andy, despite the bond he'd formed with Lisa, agreed to end all contact with the couple. They spent some time discussing the future of their relationship and explored the possibility of further polyamorous experiences, but as time progressed neither of them wanted to risk their own relationship for the sake of insatiable lust.

Ten months later and, rather than growing closer as an exclusive couple as Lena had hoped, it seems the couple have drifted further and further apart.

'We hardly touch each other these days, let alone anything else. I can't remember the last time we made love. Before we met Martin and Lisa we were at it like bunnies.' She smiles, though tears are still welling in her eyes, and then she shrugs and refills her almost empty glass once again, frowning as the last of the red wine trickles to not even half full.

'What makes you think he wants someone else?'

'I think he still wants Lisa. It's like you were saying earlier about having a deep connection with someone – Andy and Lisa had that, it was so obvious. It wasn't just sex, they fell in love. That's why I got so upset; you hit the nail on the head. They enjoyed great sex because they were soul mates – they even loved the same cheesy music for goodness sake, Robbie Williams and Girls Aloud.'

'Nothing wrong with a bit of Girls Aloud – I have a compilation DVD of theirs; I watch it with the sound turned down.'

Lena chuckles again.

'Yes, I think a lot of blokes do that!' Lena gazes into her glass for a moment, then fixes me with an intense stare. 'I just couldn't compete with the connection they formed and I don't want to feel like I'm in some kind of competition anyway. I want to feel cherished again. I feel like I've lumbered him with the booby prize and he thinks the same, that's why he doesn't come near me now. That's what you get for opening Pandora's Box I suppose.'

Watching her struggle to control her sadness, I'm tempted to reveal the real reason for my presence here this evening, to reassure her that Andy clearly has some feelings for her, but my responsibility is first and foremost to my client so I say nothing. Lena falls silent too, apparently lost in her own regrets. As 3 a.m. approaches we make a move to leave. The clone of Marlene left the pub a couple of hours ago refreshed with yet another coat of scarlet on her lips and arm-in-arm with a middle-aged man about three inches shorter than her, wearing a leather jacket and a perm Noddy Holder would be proud of. The skinny, ponytailed fellow obviously failed to impress.

I wait with Lena outside the pub and see her safely into a cab.

'It's been lovely talking to you, David. Sorry I spent most of the evening crying over you.'

'No problem. I carry more secrets around in my head than a Catholic priest.' She smiles a little at that. I kiss her lightly on the cheek and she squeezes my arm affectionately before closing the cab door and giving me a final wave as the cab pulls out onto Lower Richmond Road and does a U-turn, swinging with the grace of a racing hound and heading towards Putney Bridge.

I debate whether to call Andy now to tell him how unhappy Lena is and how in love with him she seems to be, but decide there's time enough for that in the morning. I'm not even sure I should go into that much detail with him anyway – he may be the client but I feel Lena revealed more to me this evening than she has with anyone, perhaps in a long time, and I don't want to sell her down the river for the price of a night's honeytrapping. All Andy needs to know is that she remained faithful to him and wasn't interested in taking things with me any further than chatting. Whether he decides to spend his life with Lena is not my business. I head home hoping things work out for her though – I liked her a lot.

It's 7.30 a.m. and I've already been at the office for over an hour. I got home at 4 a.m., far too late to contemplate writing my report for Andy, but I needed to get it written and delivered to him this morning, partly as I'm starting work on a new case requiring three days' surveillance today and also, I can't get Lena's distress out of my head. I'm hoping once I've completed my report and delivered the verdict to Andy I can put it behind me and leave them both to sort out their own problems.

As it happens I end up scrapping the report. Andy rings before I've written twenty words and tells me he's spent the last three hours in deep conversation with Lena. There were lots of tears and revelations, but they seem to have broken through a barrier they've spent the past ten months constructing and as he talks Lena is wrapped around him, listening to our conversation.

Lena cried all the way home in the cab this morning and a puzzled Andy, who had been waiting up for her, found himself paying an even more puzzled cab driver and supporting her inside, where she sobbed in his arms and told him she knew it was over. At first he jumped to the conclusion that the honeytrap had worked and she'd fallen for my cheesy lines, but then she told him to go to Lisa – she knew that's what he wanted and she could bear it no longer.

He dragged her into the sitting room, sat her on the sofa, kneeled in front of her and proposed to her all over again. He told her he loved her with a passion he couldn't explain and he wanted no one else – only her for the rest of his life. It turns out they'd both been paralysed by their own fears of inadequacy and rejection since their split with Martin and Lisa, and since distancing themselves from the polyamory scene, where couples agree to share not only physical but also emotional ties with another couple, neither of them could quite believe they went so far as to realise what they now wish had remained fantasy for the bedroom only.

I tell Andy how pleased I am for them both. Last night's events seem to have been the catalyst they needed to start their relationship afresh. I have a quick word with Lena, who tells me how cheeky she thinks I was to try and pull a honeytrap on her, but she says it with affection and I doubt she'll hold any grudges.

'And since I now know your true identity I wonder if you could have a chat with a friend of mine?' Lena tells me a TV presenter friend of hers, Rachel, has been having problems at home and was talking only yesterday of contacting a private detective. I tell Lena I'd be happy for her to pass my details to Rachel and wonder what on earth she may be into – if it's anything like Lena and Andy's recent hobby I'm guessing I'm in for another colourful mission.

Four days later, Rachel gets in touch and asks to see me immediately. Which is why, despite feeling exhausted after seventy-two hours of surveillance, I'm now sitting in the lounge of the beautiful home she shares with her famous footballer husband.

To my relief, I discover her problem isn't quite as colourful as I thought. Rachel is worried about the nanny she's recently hired to watch her two children. She tells me a little about herself and the family. She and her husband, Simon, are no ordinary couple. Simon is a professional footballer, playing midfield for one of the top Premiership teams. He is also good enough to have been selected for his national side. Simon was educated at public school, so doesn't fit the stereotypical image of a footballer. Rachel is a television presenter – not the MTV or game-show hostess type, but a current affairs, documentary, investigative journalist.

In other words, two educated, media-savvy and very busy people. Simon travels all over Europe fortnightly with his team in the Champions League or UEFA Cup and international football. Because he is eloquent and a student of the game (he took his UEFA 'B' licence at a young age), he finds himself much in demand as a pundit when his match commitments allow him the time.

Rachel is regularly filming, broadcasting and writing for the variety of television and radio programmes she is engaged with, not to mention her Sunday paper column. Although beautiful, she regularly turns down modelling and advertising work to maintain her serious edge, believing there are too many male colleagues ready to accuse her of dumbing down, if given half the chance.

After the birth of their first child, Hannah, Rachel took a short break from broadcasting but decided full-time motherhood was not enough to fulfil her. By the time Daniel was born a year later, Rachel was keen to return to work and enjoy the chance to mix with grown-ups again. Although the couple adore their children, both Simon and Rachel's careers are at risk of being suddenly curtailed for different reasons, and they want to make the most of their opportunities while they still can, for as long as possible.

Initially, Rachel's sister looked after the children, but after she married and moved away they decided their only option was to employ a nanny. They advertised in one of the classier publications and after wading through many responses, paper-sifting several and interviewing a few, they decided on Minnie.

Minnie made a big impression on them. She had impeccable references and was eloquent and enthusiastic throughout the interview. On introduction to the children she got down on her knees and within ten minutes Daniel and Hannah were playing happily beside her, immediately forming a bond with Minnie. They appeared to be captivated by the way she interacted with them; needless to say she passed the interview with flying colours.

Soon after the interview she moved in with the family and Simon and Rachel were able to fully explore their burgeoning but diverse careers. All was well initially; the children seemed happy and the house was impeccable, even though cleaning was not part of Minnie's duties. Simon and Rachel were more than happy with the arrangements.

But about three months into Minnie's employment things started to concern Rachel. She couldn't put her finger on anything specific; it was just a feeling that all was not well. Tiny little incidences, barely worth mentioning, began to crop up. Daniel had a small cut on his hand and couldn't tell her how it had happened, and recently Rachel's rocking horse had been broken. Of course, broken toys weren't unusual in the world of small children, but this was rather a sturdy rocking horse and Rachel couldn't understand how it could have been damaged if the children were playing properly.

On occasion, Rachel would mention her worries to Simon but on saying them aloud she realised how petty they sounded and feared she was becoming a little jealous of the time Minnie was spending with the children instead of her.

One evening, as Rachel was preparing for a night out at a television awards ceremony, she was stepping into the imperative little black dress when she called out to Simon to fetch a particular necklace from her jewellery box on the dressing table, since she was already running a little late. He knew the necklace she wanted; he had bought it for her himself. It was a diamond necklace, very simple but beautiful, bought in Hatton Garden to celebrate their third wedding anniversary a few years earlier. He went to the jewellery box but after searching for a few minutes he was unable to find it. Rachel was perplexed and a little irritated with her husband and his 'boy looks' – she knew the necklace was there a few days earlier.

In a hurry, she decided to go with the pearl necklace and matching earrings left on the shelf in her dressing room instead, but after having a quick look in the jewellery box herself and being unable to find the diamond one, she spent the evening thinking about where it could be. And then the unthinkable occurred to her: maybe Minnie had damaged it in some way while cleaning in the bedroom and had hidden it in a panic.

The following day she spoke to Minnie, who denied all knowledge of its whereabouts. Rachel was annoyed with herself for having such thoughts, but was still at a loss to explain the necklace's disappearance.

A few days later, Rachel returned home early from work. She drove her Mercedes convertible into the driveway of their large, detached home in Surrey's commuter belt, parking at the side of the house. Simon had promised Daniel and Hannah they could help with car-washing on Saturday, so she parked as close as possible to the hosepipe, but knew during the shampoo and wax tomorrow she'd be safely inside with a good book. Two small children and a hosepipe were best kept out of the way in her opinion – it was Simon's idea, so he could take care of it!

Minnie had been provided with the use of a small hatchback to transport the children and it was parked around the corner in front of the double garage. The time was 3 p.m. Rachel took her time getting out of the car as she was listening to the news on Five Live. When she eventually opened the driver's door she heard two car doors slam. Rachel rounded the corner to see the hatchback just disappearing from view as it left the driveway. She caught Minnie's eye and waved as she drove out and Minnie gave an awkward wave back and an attempt at a smile, but it was not the usual smile with a sparkle in her eyes that Rachel had become used to. As the vehicle turned onto the road, Rachel caught sight of some blue denim low down in the front of the car, as though someone was hunched over in the passenger seat.

Rachel began to feel very uneasy: first the missing necklace and now this questionable incident. As she entered the sitting room, she saw the sofa cushions were out of place. A dirty mug was left on the coffee table, a minor irritation to Rachel since she preferred coffee cups to be removed after use, but what disturbed her most was the second dirty mug down beside the sofa, on the carpet. It was the Arsenal mug Simon's brother, Uncle Stuart, had given little Daniel for Christmas as a joke, since Simon played for a rival team. Simon would place the mug at the back of the cupboard in mock disgust, but Daniel found it highly funny when his mummy presented daddy with tea in the Arsenal mug. Rachel was confused: why were there two dirty coffee cups in the lounge? The children, as far as she was aware, weren't partial to Nescafe, and Minnie was supposed to let Rachel know if she was inviting friends over.

Deciding not to touch anything, Rachel went upstairs to shower and change. She knew Minnie and the children would be home soon, after Minnie had collected them from afternoon nursery at 3.15 p.m. As she soaped herself she made up her mind not to say anything, *yet*.

By the time Rachel had dressed and arrived downstairs, Minnie and the children were home. Rachel checked the sitting room and was a little unnerved to find the sofa cushions spaced at regular, almost precise intervals, as if no one had sat down all day. There was no sign of the coffee mugs either. After cuddling the kids and playing with them for a while, Rachel went into the kitchen. One of the two mugs was in the sink waiting to be washed, but the other wasn't with it. Rachel opened the cupboard where the mugs were usually kept and found the Arsenal mug in there, washed and dried, although the handle was still slightly damp.

Rachel found Minnie's behaviour a little sinister. OK, it was only a mug, but the clandestine manner in which Minnie carried on unnerved her. The following evening when Simon got back from Amsterdam after his team's match against Ajax, Rachel told him her concerns, but he dismissed them as the overactive imaginations of an investigative journalist. Simon's team had lost the match 2–1, with Simon making a vital error of judgement that led to one of the goals against them, and Rachel initially felt that Simon's dismissive tone was borne out of his frustration. He was always in a bad mood for a couple of days after a match loss; she usually spent Saturday afternoon on tenterhooks, praying for a good result. She couldn't blame Simon. Perfectionism was one of the traits they shared and no doubt one of the reasons they were initially attracted to one another. They both shared a love of books, but if anyone borrowed a copy and turned the corner over to mark the page it drove them wild. Their DVD collection was stored in alphabetical order and if a CD was put in the wrong cover, well, both of them would be up in arms. In that way they were ideally suited: the perfect match.

Rachel tried to put her worries out of her mind – work was going to become frantically busy over the next few weeks and she needed to keep her composure. As time went on, however, the dull tinkling of distant fears grew and full-tone alarm bells started ringing. Daniel, usually a happy, talkative three-year-old, began to chatter less. He developed a minor stutter and became very clingy in the mornings when Rachel was ready to leave for work, crying and cuddling Rachel as though worried she'd never return.

One evening, as Rachel was putting Daniel to bed, she reached up to swat a moth away and Daniel cowered, instantly putting his hands up to protect his face.

'What's the matter, Daniel?'

Daniel said nothing but began to cry.

'It's all right, sweetie.' Rachel rocked and soothed him and he was soon quietened, but his cowering action hadn't passed her by; that was reflex, she was sure of it. Perhaps a child at the nursery was bullying him? Her first thought was to talk to Minnie about it in the morning, but something stopped her – some primeval instinct she wasn't aware she possessed. She decided to call a private detective instead.

Enter yours truly. As Rachel tells me her concerns, I wonder how on earth she keeps her house so immaculate with two small children running around. Her lounge looks like a showroom for Habitat. Everything is beige, from the cubic beige-leather sofas to the thick beige carpet beneath our feet. Either Hannah and Daniel are impeccably behaved robots, or Rachel has this entire room refurnished every few months.

'Do you think I'm being paranoid?' asks Rachel, as she takes a sip of coffee and places the mug carefully on a beige-leather coaster.

'Women's intuition, in my experience, is usually right,' I say. I don't want to worry her, but I don't want to play down her concerns either. 'With your permission, I'd like to set up surveillance cameras around the house so I can watch what Minnie's up to when you're not here. It could be she's perfectly innocent.'

Rachel nods, looking worried.

'The cameras… they won't damage the wallpaper, will they?'

It's a fiddly, time-consuming job to install the surveillance equipment, since I have to take so much care not to leave any marks or scratches anywhere, and I begin to worry I won't be finished before Minnie returns from her day shopping with the children. But by 4 p.m. everything is installed and operational. If Minnie really is a rat, the trap is ready for her.

Two days later, I have a dynamite film to show Rachel. I've cut and spliced footage from all over the house, so Rachel can see the 'highlights' of Minnie's behaviour and we sit together in my office and watch the blockbuster on my laptop. The only thing that's missing is popcorn.

There are no opening credits, of course, but scene one is explosive. Within minutes it's clear the 'movie' we're watching isn't *Mary Poppins*. For a start, Mary Poppins wouldn't leave small children unsupervised while she tried on their mother's clothes and jewellery. While Minnie is modelling Rachel's wardrobe, Hannah and Daniel are running wild around the house. We watch as, giggling, they flush the toilet over and over again, hurl themselves down the stairs and squabble over toys. No wonder Hannah's rocking horse broke – the kids are playing very rough, stamping on toys, books and colouring pencils.

Rachel can barely watch. She's sat next to me with hands over her face, peeping through her fingers.

After an hour of nerve-wracking footage, during which Daniel finds a bottle of bleach in the bathroom and chews at the lid and Hannah turns the cooker repeatedly on and off, Minnie emerges from the bedroom and leaves the house.

'No prizes for guessing how Daniel cut his hand,' I say. 'He probably found something sharp to play with, and Minnie wasn't there to take it off him.'

'She's leaving the house!' Rachel says. 'That terrible woman. That terrible, terrible woman. How can she leave two small children alone? I can't bear this.'

But there are more surprises to come.

Minnie returns with a tall, slim man with a craggy face and warm, brown eyes.

'That's Jimmy!' says Rachel. 'Our neighbour.'

We watch as the pair disappear into Rachel and Simon's bedroom, and I leave it up to Rachel's imagination to work out what's happening. I do, of course, have footage of what went on, but I didn't want to turn this movie into a top-shelf affair.

'But he's *married*,' says Rachel, in horror. 'I thought he and Denise were made for each other. What on earth is he thinking?'

The film plays on, and shows the children playing in Hannah's bedroom. We watch as Hannah takes Rachel's diamond necklace out from under her bed and holds it up to the window. Daniel makes a grab for it, but Hannah keeps it out of his reach, gazing in awe as the light hits the sparkling gems. Then she tucks it safely under the bed again, and she and Daniel begin jumping on the mattress.

'So there is some good news,' says Rachel, dryly. 'At least Minnie's not a thief.'

But the grand finale is still to come. When the kids start banging on Rachel's bedroom door, a half-naked Minnie comes out and smacks them both hard around the head, before dragging them down the corridor and dumping them in Hannah's bedroom. They both sit there, crying and howling, until half an hour later Jimmy sneaks out of the house and Minnie takes the children to nursery.

'It was Jimmy,' says Rachel, as if she's just solved a great mystery. 'He must have been the one hiding in the back of her car, that time. Lord knows why he didn't just go home – maybe Denise was there and he should have been at work.'

She jumps to her feet.

'She's supposed to be picking them up from nursery in an hour. I'd better get a move on.' She sighs and puts her head in her hands. 'Christ, I've got that dinner tonight. I'll just have to tell them I'm ill. There's no way that woman is spending another minute around my children.'

A few days later, Rachel phones me with an update.

'Monstrous Minnie has gone,' she tells me, 'but we're a bit stuck without a nanny. Work have given me compassionate leave, but I'm dying to get back to the TV studio.' There's a pause. 'You must think I'm a terrible mother.'

'Of course not,' I reassure her. 'I'm just glad the kids are safe and happy again.'

Bringing up children is the most demanding and difficult task in the world. I take my hat off to those who manage to do it well. Couple this with the demands of surviving financially and it becomes an almost impossible task. There are many couples up and down the country who cannot make ends meet without both working full-time.

Some manage this with a little help, maybe from a relative. However, many turn to 'professional' help and employ a nanny. Nannies come in all shapes, sizes, nationalities, abilities and personalities. It is one of those things that is a mystery to me. Why do people do it? Yes I know; the cost of mortgages, running a home, car and, if you're lucky, having a bit of a social life or holiday, all need money; the choice of one parent working and one staying at home with the little ones is not an option for many couples.

What I can't understand is why perfectly reasonable, well-educated adults suddenly lose all sense of reason when trying to get care for their most precious possessions: their own children. Now before the graduates of Norland College and similarly qualified professionals take offence, I'm not referring to specialist carers dedicated to a career in childcare. No, I'm referring to the phenomenon of employing a girl (or boy) from Eastern Europe. The Internet is awash with agencies offering a 'find a nanny service' or 'nanny matching', but there is often little or no screening and the applicants are not even interviewed in person. There are ample opportunities to fabricate credentials and qualifications. Parents receive a CV emailed through an agency and a decision is made based on sketchy information. Often a complete stranger, with varying degrees of English ability, is employed to look after little Emily or James.

The couple arrange to pick up their new employee from Stansted after their easyJet flight has arrived, having flown in from somewhere they've never heard of and they try to assess on the journey home whether they can entrust their home, valuables, car and, most importantly, their children to them. Very soon afterwards they hop on the train to London, head for the office and spend the rest of the day, and probably many others, worrying about how their decision is playing out at home.

I couldn't do it. Maybe I'm a touch more cynical than others. My world revolves around deceit, violence, dishonesty, infidelity, selfishness and some vices that would curl your toes, so I may be a little biased. But I can't help thinking that leaving your children daily with someone you don't know has a touch of recklessness to it. I've witnessed first-hand the guilt experienced by parents when their actions and choices have resulted in pain and upset for their children. As Elizabeth Stone said, 'Making the decision to have a child is momentous. It is to decide forever to have your heart go walking around outside your body.'

Rachel and Simon were lucky – they detected changes in their children's behaviour early enough to intervene before anything too serious occurred, but not all episodes of child neglect or abuse end this way. I'm often tempted to start a campaign for the use of private detectives in cases where children are placed on the at-risk register, if only to provide equipment to monitor the behaviour of parents or other carers. I believe it would be reasonable action to take to install 'nanny-cams' in the homes of children who are thought to be at risk – it should be a condition attached to allowing parents to keep custody of their children. First it would prevent any further abuse taking place, and second it would allow social services to monitor and intervene if any episodes appear to be of concern to them – a cross between *Big Brother* and *Supernanny*.

Some may say it's an impingement on the civil rights of these parents, but I say, so what? I don't believe genuine parents who want their children to remain in their own family would object. And surely being monitored in this way is better than the alternative? Having a child hurt, or even killed, is the most heartbreaking thing any parent could ever comprehend.

In the light of events with Baby P, supposedly 'protected' by Haringey Social Services, I think it would be a huge step forward in reducing child cruelty. Bearing in mind one child a week in the

UK dies at the hands of those responsible for protecting them I don't think the general public would object.

Even though I'm a seasoned PI I'm still shocked by the level of cruelty to which some 'human beings' will stoop. Of course, when children are involved it's particularly upsetting but it's not unusual for me to shed a tear or two on behalf of some of my adult clients. When the perpetrator of a heartless act is a woman I find it all the more disturbing. I think it's because most people, me included, tend to view women as the 'fairer sex'. No matter how many times I witness female infidelity I still manage to feel a little shocked by it.

Take Cheri, for example. Her partner, a celebrity on the UK professional wrestling circuit, contacted me a few years ago, desperate to know if he could trust Cheri, his then girlfriend, after the press printed details of her cheating on him with another wrestler: a famous 'bad boy', who played the pantomime villain during wrestling matches.

Cheri swore to my client, who was known as Greg in his free time, that everything was finished and she'd never cheat again. But Greg's trust was shattered, and he knew he could only continue the relationship if he had conclusive proof she wasn't tempted by other men. He asked me to visit a local bar where Cheri worked and set a honeytrap. No problem, or so I thought.

But as it turned out, things were much more difficult than I'd anticipated. The bar Cheri worked in was a cross between a pub and a strip club, which meant that talking to the girls behind the bar was near impossible. Every hour, Cheri and the other barmaids would jump up on tables and perform sexy dances, which meant none of them were short of male attention. Talking to Cheri directly meant risking a black eye from the two burly bald men buying her shots, so I had to resort to plan B and wait until she'd clocked off for the night and see if I could whisk her away for a drink after work.

Kicking-out time rolled around, but Cheri didn't look ready to wind down for the evening. I watched her apply a generous coating of lipstick as the other barmaids ushered out the last of the customers, me included. It didn't look like I was going to get to talk to Cheri that evening, despite my long wait, but as I was being shooed out I noticed three men in the corner who weren't being asked to leave.

'Is there a lock-in tonight?' I asked the petite, skinny blonde with very obvious breast implants, who was politely walking me towards the door. The girl giggled.

'A lock-in?' She looked over her shoulder at the other barmaid, a well-seasoned forty-something woman with piercing blue eyes, jet-black waist-length hair and a killer figure. The woman gave her the tiniest nod, and the blonde girl whispered:

'You mean a gentleman's night?'

I nodded, as if I knew what she meant.

'Fifty pounds to join. And then you and the lady decide extra charges between yourselves.'

She looked me up and down, smiled, and then guided me towards the back booth where I paid her fifty pounds in crisp tens from my wallet. It was a charge that would be added to my client's expenses, but I thought it highly likely Greg would want me to find out what was going on tonight.

I sat with the three other men, all of them past forty, overweight and glugging beer in a restless, impatient way. They were obviously waiting for something to happen, but of course I didn't know what that was.

There was a clunk as the bar door was locked. Then Cheri and the other two barmaids came and arranged themselves around the room, the blonde girl stretched out on a cushioned bench, the black-haired woman sat backwards on a chair with her legs spread like a cowboy and Cheri perched on the bar with her bare legs crossed.

The men around me struggled to their feet, and one of them pushed past and lumbered towards the blonde girl.

I worked out pretty quickly it was a free-for-all: whoever approached a girl first got to talk to her, and from what I gathered, do a lot more than that if he wanted to.

In two strides I'd made it over to Cheri. The hidden camera on my lapel was running, and I knew it would capture every expression on her face as we spoke. At the moment, it was filming serious 'come to bed' eyes, outlined in heavy kohl.

'Hi,' Cheri said as I approached, uncrossing her legs and crossing them the other way. It took all my self-control not to gulp like a little schoolboy, but instead I leaned nonchalantly on the bar beside her.

'Hello. You OK?'

Cheri smiled, probably used to men not at all sure how to behave around her.

'I'm fine,' she said, calmly. 'You?'

'What's on offer?' I asked – an innocent enough question at a bar under normal circumstances, but right then it was laden with meaning. All thoughts of making a personal connection based on her hobbies and interests (which Greg told me were kittens and dry-slope skiing) were now firmly at the back of my mind.

Cheri leaned forward and whispered in my ear. When she'd finished whispering, I was quite sure the lens of my film camera must have steamed up; she'd offered me quite a few things, and none of them were drinks. I decided to play the very intimidated, very British customer and pretend to bottle out.

'Sorry,' I spluttered, 'I've got to go.'

I headed towards the door, and Cheri, to her credit, followed and politely opened the locks. 'See you again,' she said, running her dainty hand along my bicep and then giving it a firm squeeze. 'I'll look out for you.' She gave me a dazzling smile as I stumbled onto the street, then closed the painted, wooden doors behind me and I heard the clunk of heavy locks falling back into place.

I phoned Greg first thing the next day, and we arranged to meet at his office: a tiny, breeze block-lined room inside the gym were he worked by day as a fitness instructor, before his wrestler alter-ego took over at night.

I'd brought the film footage with me, but as it turned out Greg was too distressed to see it. As soon as I explained about the 'gentleman's night' and the services Cheri had offered me, he burst into tears. I'd never seen a big, fake-tanned muscle man cry before, and I haven't since, but Greg cried that day like a teenage boy who'd just had his heart broken. He wanted to know everything: who else had been at the bar, what the other girls looked like, the exact services Cheri had offered… but he couldn't bear to see footage of her propped on the bar soliciting for business. That was a step too far.

Several months later, the papers reported that Cheri was yet again seeing her former lover, the 'bad boy' wrestler, but had also been seen leaving a hotel with a well-known local businessman. Greg was lucky to find out about Cheri when he did. I'm not saying all women who offer sex for sale are serial adulterers. In fact, I've met ladies of the night who are incredibly faithful to their partners once their working day is done. But a woman who can repeatedly deceive her partner is showing little respect for him or their relationship together, and ultimately it was the betrayal that upset Greg more than anything else.

EPILOGUE

Richard continues to solve concerns for clients of his private detective agency. He realises these services can be financially out of reach for some, and so he has provided further detailed useful tips on how you can be your own private detective on his website: www.ex-da.com.

He is often invited to talk on various radio shows about his truth-finding services and in particular his honeytrapping service, which he has also written a song about titled 'Honeytrapper, the Sexpionage song', available from iTunes (where you can hear Richard sing his intriguing song).

Richard aims to constantly review his services to cater for the ever ingenious ways that his targets use to hide their immoral ways. This includes the option of Richard taking his clients up in a light aircraft (using his private pilot's licence) to monitor their cheating partners from the air if required.

Richard hopes that his services can continue to help solve the issues that cause his clients heartache; as he says, the heart is like our planet Earth: we only have one and we need to prevent it being polluted with unnecessary garbage!

ACKNOWLEDGEMENTS

To my wonderful mum... I am forever grateful for your constant care, and will always cherish you.

To my amazing pops... Thanks for being a cool daddio. Your advice and influence have been priceless.

To my magical daughter and her mother... You have fulfilled a dream, and I look to help you both reach yours.

To my relatives here in the UK and on/around the Rock of Gibraltar, especially Emilio, Derrick, Alan and Mikey... *La sangre es más espesa que el agua.*

To Flt/Lt Jimbo Winter and every Commanding Officer, staff and cadet who had the stress of having me on their squadron... *Per Ardua ad Astra.*

To my school mates and teachers/lecturers, especially Miss Williams and Mr Clegg... Who'd have thought it, and yes we should appreciate our teachers/lecturers more.

To my ghostwriter Petrina Brown and my publisher... Great job helping write and publish this book, and hope this mention helps you both produce more books.

To my past and future PI customers, as well as PI Arrabella of Minx... Thank you for using Expedite Detective Agency, which I trust helped you to find the truth and better times.

COMPETITION TO WIN A PRIVATE DETECTIVE KIT!

Richard Martinez uses various surveillance devices in the course of his private investigations throughout this book. Can you find 20 of them?

The winner will receive their own private detective kit from Richard Martinez including rear-view sunglasses, professional fingerprinting detection kit and a wireless mini spy camera.

To enter the draw, go to www.summersdale.com and click on the competitions link on the homepage.

Terms and conditions apply

REAL CRIME SCENE INVESTIGATIONS

Forensic Experts Reveal Their Secrets

CONNIE FLETCHER

REAL CRIME SCENE INVESTIGATIONS
Forensic Experts Reveal Their Secrets
Connie Fletcher

ISBN: 978 1 84024 530 1   Paperback   £9.99

Forensic science is increasingly important in solving crime, and millions of people all over the world are captivated by the TV programmes *CSI: Miami* and *CSI: New York* currently being shown on Channel 5.

In this fascinating book, experts such as homicide detectives, forensic scientists and crime lab specialists reveal the stories behind their most challenging cases. Just what secrets can a decomposed corpse reveal? Discover how an investigator found grounds for conviction in a single fibre as long as a fingernail.

Forensic science is not just fingerprints and DNA, it's also blood splatter patterns, footprints, minute indentations, dust patterns - every contact leaves a trace. From the first examination of a crime scene through to the final court case, discover the painstaking efforts of true-life experts as they search for evidence against society's most dangerous criminals. The result is more fascinating than fiction.

'*You can watch* CSI *for sheer entertainment, but if reality is important to you, read this book. Connie Fletcher has assembled actual stories from the real homicide cops, crime scene investigators, and support folks who tell it like it really is, in their own words. It's an easy read, full of reality*'
Captain Ray Peavy, Homicide Bureau Commander, Los Angeles County

'*Right on the mark. This book pertains to the real world of murder investigation as opposed to the perception created by CSI*'
Vernon J. Geberth, Commander of Bronx Homicide (Ret.), NYPD

SECRET
SOCIETIES

Their Mysteries Revealed

JOHN LAWRENCE REYNOLDS

SECRET SOCIETIES
Their Mysteries Revealed

John Lawrence Reynolds

ISBN: 978 1 84024 612 4   Paperback   £8.99

Secret societies have flourished throughout history, capturing the public imagination and generating fear, suspicion and above all fascination. Reynolds treats the reader to a behind-the-scenes look at the origins, initiations, secret signs and famous members of the most notorious secret societies of all time. Included are chapters on the Cosa Nostra, Al Qaeda, the Triads, the Assassins, the Yakuza, Kabbalah, the Freemasons and the Druids.

Does a global power actually control the election of world leaders? Are some secret societies little more than a group of boys playing at secret handshakes? Based on exhaustive research, with an emphasis on authenticity rather than speculation, *Secret Societies* will grip readers from the opening page.

Have you enjoyed this book? If so, why not write a review on your favourite website?

Thank you very much for buying this Summersdale book.

www.summersdale.com